EVEN EAGLES
NEED A PUSH

EVEN EAGLES NEED A PUSH

LEARNING TO SOAR
IN A CHANGING WORLD

DAVID McNALLY

TransForm Press

International Standard Book Number: 0-9626921-0-7
Library of Congress Catalog Card Number: 90-0700697

TransForm Press, 7500 Flying Cloud Drive, Eden Prairie, Minnesota 55344

Printed in the United States of America

10   9   8   7   6   5   4

To My Mother
JESSIE
Who Gave Me Confidence

To My Father
DAVID
Who Taught Me To Give

To My Children
SARAH, KATE, SEAN, JESSIE, & BETH
Who Give Me Joy

To My Wife
JO
Who Teaches Me Love

Many people gave their precious time to read and
comment on the ever evolving manuscript of this book. Their insights,
honesty, and suggestions contributed significantly to the finished work.
To all of them I am most grateful and honored by their participation.

In the beginning Ron Lehmann was my editor. He offered
encouragement, the advice of a true professional, and his wonderful
sense of humor. My agent, Jonathon Lazear, convinced
me I had something worthy to say, which boosted my
sometimes sagging spirit. My associate, Sandi Heaberlin, magically
transferred my often illegible writing onto the computer.
David Martin did the final edit with sensitivity and wisdom, which were
the perfect match for any insecurities I had as a writer.

My vision was brought to life by that wonderfully creative organization,
Herman∗Mancino, of Minneapolis. They designed
both the cover and layout of the pages. Through the artistic talent of
Lisa Etziony, the printed word began to breathe.

Finally, there are the people whose support and belief in me
make my work possible: my wife, Jo, my confidants, Mary Regnier and
Frank Plant, and those throughout the world who I am privileged
to call friends.

ACKNOWLEDGEMENTS

CONTENTS

T
O THE READER FROM THE AUTHOR:

A short time ago I became aware rather abruptly of my primary goal as a parent. My eldest child turned sixteen and with a loud cry of "free at last" she got her driver's license. My fears were somewhat allayed by the assurance of her driving instructor: "Don't worry. Your daughter is very confident."

I realized there was no other single human quality that more affected the outcomes of our lives than confidence. Only with confidence do we advance boldly in the direction of our dreams. Only with confidence do we tackle life's challenges with the faith that we can handle them. As each of my children eventually leave the family nest, I am convinced there is no greater gift with which they could depart than confidence.

This is not, however, a quality I see rampant in the world. In these wondrous times of change and opportunity, some people are happily riding the momentum of the megatrends, exclaiming with John Naisbitt, "What a fantastic time to be alive." But there are many others who agree with Woody Allen's statement: "Most of the time I don't have much fun, and the rest of the time I don't have any fun at all."

It seems that lack of confidence remains a malaise that is still preventing a disproportionate number of incredibly talented people from fully participating in, and contributing to, what for the first time may be the attainable goals of global peace and prosperity. This lack of confidence, on all levels, has got to stop, for the world needs each of us, in our own special way, both to embrace and be committed to these most worthy goals.

This book, therefore, is dedicated to confidence—great confidence, your great confidence. Its purpose is to inspire you to live the life that perhaps, until now, you had only imagined for yourself. Its mission is to give you the tools to create that life so that, no matter the obstacles along the way, you know you have what it takes to surmount them.

The path we shall follow is not one laden with positive platitudes, but rather it is a quest for insight, wholeness, and integrity. We shall embark upon a journey of discovery, to reflect upon and clarify what is truly important and meaningful to you. Specifically, we shall be seeking answers to three of life's most important questions:

Why are you here?

What do you have to contribute that will make a difference?

What do you value and believe in?

Confident people have a philosophy about why they were created. They have a sense of purpose, a belief that they are important, that their lives matter.

Confident people know what they bring to the

world. They are aware of what they are good at, their special abilities. They know that success, satisfaction, and fulfillment are the rewards for contributing their gifts and talents toward something that makes a difference.

Confident people know that the accomplishment of any worthwhile endeavor requires commitment. They know that it is only to that in which they truly value and believe are they willing to be committed.

The process we shall follow is analogous to a "time out." You will be investing time reviewing and developing new strategies for your life. You will be resting, catching your breath, breaking the momentum of runaway negative influences, refocusing and re-energizing. You will be aligning yourself mentally, physically, emotionally, and spiritually to ensure each part of you is working together to win this game called life.

Many of the questions you will be asking do not have easy answers. It is important, therefore, that you not be locked into the structure of the book. If at any-time you prefer to read on and return to the exercises at a later time, you are absolutely free to do so. Do not feel confined to the form I have created; do what works for you. After all, discovering what is best for you is one of our primary objectives.

Most of us have heard a great deal about the importance of motivation in getting what you want from life. The payoff for your commitment to completing the exercises and processes will be to move you to a level even more powerful than motivation. It is called inspiration.

To be inspired means to move forward with purpose and enthusiasm. Purpose denotes a clarity of intention while enthusiasm is derived from the Greek *en theos,* a god or spirit within. Clarity of intention propelled by a spirit within is the most potent combination for achievement and creativity known to humankind.

Inspired persons know why they do what they do and why they want what they want. They are not shackled by the pettiness that restrains so many lives. The inspired person comes to life with a purpose and passion, with the daily desire to grow and contribute.

If that's what you want, then let's spend some time together.

The eagle gently coaxed her offspring toward the edge of the nest. Her heart quivered with conflicting emotions as she felt their resistance to her persistent nudging. "Why does the thrill of soaring have to begin with the fear of falling?" she thought. This ageless question was still unanswered for her.

As in the tradition of the species, her nest was located high on the shelf of a sheer rock face. Below there was nothing but air to support the wings of each child. "Is it possible that this time it will not work?" she thought. Despite her fears, the eagle knew it was time. Her parental mission was all but complete. There remained one final task—the push.

The eagle drew courage from an innate wisdom. Until her children discovered their wings, there was no purpose for their lives. Until they learned how to soar, they would fail to understand the privilege it was to have been born an eagle. The push was the greatest gift she had to offer. It was her supreme act of love. And so one by one she pushed them, and they flew!

David McNally

June 1990

To Begin Again

Renewal

Chapter
1

Jimmy's mother called out to him at seven in the morning, "Jimmy, get up. It's time for school." There was no answer. She called again, this time more loudly, "Jimmy, get up! It's time for school!" Once more there was no answer. Exasperated, she went to his room and shook him saying, "Jimmy, it's time to get ready for school."

He answered, "Mother, I'm not going to school. There's fifteen hundred kids at that school and every one of them hates me. I'm not going to school."

"Get to school!" she replied sharply.

"But, Mother, all the teachers hate me, too. I saw three of them talking the other day and one of them was pointing his finger at me. I know they all hate me so I'm not going to school," Jimmy answered.

"Get to school!" his mother demanded again.

"But, Mother, I don't understand it. Why would you want to put me through all of that torture and suffering?" he protested.

"Jimmy, for two good reasons," she fired back. "First, you're forty-two years old. Secondly, you're the principal."

There are few of us who, on some days, have not felt like Jimmy. We just do not want to go to school. That school, of course, is life itself, where dropping out or playing hookey can seem a much better idea than facing the challenges that inevitably lay ahead.

Perhaps, however, you have never thought of life

Life can only be understood backwards; but it must be lived forwards.

—Soren Kirkegaard

as a school. Yet the truly memorable life, one that is celebrated with love and admiration, always has a history rich in accomplishments and experiences. Most important, inherent within those experiences are valuable lessons that greatly enhance the quality of life. Pablo Casals, the great cellist, was asked why, at eighty-five years of age, he continued to practice five hours a day. He replied, "Because I think I'm get-ting better."

To grasp the significance of this more fully, let me quickly and ruthlessly slay a dragon, a dangerous soul-destroying myth. Our culture perpetuates an illusion of success. Through the over-exposure and media attention given to the rich, powerful, and glamorous, we are seduced by appearances into the belief that some people have made it. The implica-tion, and the lie, is that they then live happily ever after. Those who have made it to "made it" discover that happily ever after doesn't exist, a realization that can be devastating.

THE ILLUSION OF "SUCCESS"

Success begins the moment we understand that life is about growing; it is about acquiring the knowl-edge and skills we need to live more fully and effec-tively. Life is meant to be a never-ending education, and when this is fully appreciated, we are no longer survivors but adventurers. Life becomes a journey of discovery, an exploration into our potential. Any joy and exuberance we experience in living are the fruits of our willingness to risk, our openness to change, and our ability to create what we want for our lives.

If you have already risked much and lost much, it doesn't matter. Mistakes don't matter. Failure doesn't matter. What matters is that you learned from your mistakes and failures. What matters is that you moved forward, you grew as a result of those experiences. The mistake-riddled life is much richer, more interesting, and more stimulating than the life that has never risked or taken a stand on anything. Hal Prince, the famous Broadway producer, said, "Anyone who hasn't had a failure is an amateur."

A successful bank president, about to retire, was being interviewed by a reporter: "Sir, to what do you attribute your success?"

"That's easy to answer: good decisions."

"And to what do you attribute your good decisions?"

"That's easier still: the wisdom gained from experience."

"And where did you get that experience?"

"Easy again: bad decisions!"

Inherent within the discoveries and experiences of your life is the wisdom upon which to build your future. This wisdom is your most important asset as you come to terms with what you honestly want for your life. On the other hand, you are destined to repeat the mistakes from which you have not learned. Let me share with you how I came to this understanding.

Life is about moving, it's about change. And when things stop doing that they're dead.

–Twyla Tharp

My own family environment was one where I was the eldest son of two very loving and ambitious parents. I inherited their ambition and decided that I was destined for success and success meant being wealthy. Impatience, combined with an intense desire, led me to forego college and start my first business straight out of high school.

Two qualities fueled my drive for success: boundless energy and knowing exactly what I wanted. I was primed and ready to take advantage of whatever business opportunity would get me to my destination fastest. I was not suspicious or afraid of "get rich quick" schemes; on the contrary, I wanted to get rich, and the quicker, the better!

In my mid-twenties my drive had propelled me to a level of success that many would regard as the American Dream fulfilled. A Rolls Royce, a beautiful country home, Europe as my playground—all of these were evidence of the fact that I had joined the ranks of those who had "made it."

At the age of twenty-eight my business failed. This was a devastating blow to a previously unchallenged ego. Having merged my whole identity with the business, when it disintegrated, so did I. Without my possessions, I not only had nothing, but it seemed I was nothing.

The downhill slide was slow and steady. I slipped in every facet of my being—physically, spiritually,

mentally, and morally. Incapable of dwelling on anything but regrets and what ifs, convinced that I had
blown the most wonderful opportunity life would
ever present, I saw no promise in the future whatsoever.

I took refuge in drinking with friends. The late
nights became so frequent that my marriage was
severely threatened. Yet, ironically, it was my wife
who rescued me.

One morning I came to the breakfast table nurs-
ing a king-sized hangover. For those of you who
understand, you know it is not a time in your life
when you are looking for advice. That preference
notwithstanding, my wife very slowly, quietly, and
succinctly uttered some words that, forever, are
imprinted in my mind.

"David, you are becoming so ordinary."

Those words blasted through the alcohol and
stayed to haunt me for the rest of the day. Deep in
my heart I knew that there was no such thing as an
ordinary human being. "What has happened to
you?" I asked myself. "Two years ago you were on
top of the world, and now you are wallowing in the
gutter!"

ONE MUST BE PREPARED TO ACCEPT INSIGHT

I believe insight comes when—and only
when—one is prepared to accept it. In this case, the
student was ready and the answers came quickly.
Like many others, I had reacted to my misfortune as

if it were just that—a function of luck, totally out of my control. I saw myself as being victimized, and so spent my time playing the victim's game—blaming, making excuses, and rationalizing. This negative mental state continually drained my energy and was the precursor of self-destructive actions that had been causing a devastating chain reaction.

My deep despair and my wife's words combined to shock me into what is known as a blinding glimpse of the obvious. So life had been unfair to me? So what? Hadn't it also been unfair to thousands—millions—of others? And hadn't many of those people faced far worse circumstances yet had absolutely refused to be defeated?

The most common responses to a life crisis are denial, resistance, and acceptance.

Denial: burying one's head in the sand hoping the problem will somehow mysteriously and painlessly disappear.

Resistance: fighting what has or is happening in a futile effort to turn back the clock or maintain the status quo.

Acceptance: not necessarily liking the situation but fully acknowledging its reality and being willing to deal with the truth of what happened no matter how severe.

Denial and resistance effectively prolong the pain, while acceptance opens the door to finding creative

Failure is, in a sense, the highway to success, inasmuch as every discovery of what is false leads us to seek earnestly after what is true.

–John Keats

solutions to the problem.

In his book, *Man's Search for Meaning,* Victor Frankl relates what he learned from his experience as a prisoner in Auschwitz. He writes, "Everything can be taken from a man but one thing: the last of the human freedoms—to choose one's attitude in any given set of circumstances, to choose one's own way."

Denial and resistance had been a part of my life for nearly two years. Victor Frankl's words inspired me to make new choices, to finally accept what had happened with all of its implications and consequences, and then to move forward using the experience as a powerful lesson upon which to build a positive future.

The decision to accept what had happened, to stop being a victim and be responsible, was not easy, but it was, unquestionably, the turning point for my recovery.

The renewal process for me began with a brutally honest assessment of my physical assets and liabilities and my personal strengths and weaknesses. I then shifted my focus from the effects of the business failure to examining why it had originally been successful. Even though I was still wiped out financially, I gradually began to see what I could do about it. The determination then slowly emerged to once again take charge of my life. Sobered by my riches to rags experience, I felt ready this time to do it right.

Over the ensuing years, I developed a successful new business. Building on my gifts for teaching and motivating others, I became the South Pacific franchisee for an international management and sales training organization. Based in Sydney, Australia, we served many of the major corporations in the region.

More important here than any tale of success, however, is the concept that a crisis is often what author and psychologist Dick Leider refers to as one of life's "wake up" calls. Crises force our attention on the disorder in our thinking and can save us as we teeter on the brink of an even greater disaster. It often takes these alarms going off before we become fully conscious of where our lives have been heading.

I now understand that all human development is determined first and foremost by one's thinking. Whether we are conscious of it, a personal philosophy of life, a way of seeing the world, a point of view, evolves over the years. We make decisions about who we are, what we believe, and what we are capable of. These decisions direct our actions and mold our behavior, the final product of which is the circumstances and conditions in which we find ourselves.

In my workshops and seminars, I still find considerable resistance to this idea. Clearly, many of us are not comfortable with accepting that we have created

CRISIS = A "WAKE-UP CALL" TO LIFE

There is no shortcut to life. To the end of our days, life is a lesson imperfectly learned.

—Harrison E. Salisbury

who we are, for this implies responsibility. It seems there is no tougher challenge that we face than to accept personal responsibility for not only what we are but also what we can be.

For any of us to be truly free—if we are to learn to soar in this changing world—we must first be willing to be responsible for our lives.

Consider the words of Vaclav Havel, when as the newly elected president of Czechoslovakia, he addressed his people shortly after they had broken free from the chains of communism. "We cannot lay all the blame on those who ruled us before, not only because this would not be true but also because it could detract from the responsibility each of us now faces—the responsibility to act on our own freely, sensibly, and quickly. . . . This, it seems to me, is the great moral stake of the present moment."

The past lives now only in your memory, but the future holds a myriad of possibilities. No matter where you find yourself at this moment you, too, can begin the renewal process. Just as your body is constantly regenerating itself physiologically, you can renew yourself mentally by replacing worn out, stagnant thinking with thoughts that stimulate a sense of hope and positive anticipation about your future.

Richard Bach, in his book *Illusions,* writes, "You are never given a wish without also being given the power to make it true." This is the shared philosophy

ACCEPTING RESPONSIBILITY FOR ONE'S LIFE

For any of us to be truly free— if we are to learn to soar in this changing world—we must first be willing to be responsible for our lives.

of those who are in charge of their lives.

In case what I'm saying, sounds Pollyannish, let me caution with a note of reality. Although the formula for learning to soar is relatively simple, the application is rarely easy. Leaving the nest requires courage and commitment. Richard Bach added to his statement: "You may have to work for it, however."

The work begins as soon as we choose a new direction for our lives, for confronting our hope and anticipation are competing thoughts of doubt and limitation. We can learn to soar only in direct proportion to our determination to rise above the doubt and transcend the limitations.

A man was hurrying back to his office, having been delayed at lunch, and now he was late for a business appointment. Out of the corner of his eye he saw something so startling that he was forced to stop and observe another man who was casually looking through a store window. After two minutes the pressure of his appointment made him continue his journey.

Later that afternoon he spoke to a colleague about his strange experience.

"Harry, have you heard that in this world everybody has an exact double?"

"Yes, I have."

Well, at lunch I was walking along the mall when I saw this guy who made me do a double take. I stopped and looked at him and finally realized he was my exact double."

"What do you mean?"

We can learn to soar only in direct proportion to our determination to rise above the doubt and transcend the limitations.

"Well, he was the same height and weight and had the same coloring and features—everything! He was dressed differently, but he was my exact double!"

"Did you go up to him and ask him who he was and where he was from?"

"No I didn't. You know, I just didn't like the look of him!"

These thoughts of doubt and limitation attack us where we are most vulnerable, feel inferior, or believe we are somehow lacking. Understand, however, that if they win, you lose, remaining stuck right where you are and fearful of exploring the potential for your life.

The thoughts of doubt and limitation sound like:

"It won't work."

"A leopard can't change its spots."

"Who do you think you are?"

"If it was possible, someone else would have done it."

"You're not smart enough."

"You can't teach an old dog new tricks."

"What will happen if you screw this up?"

"I'm happy the way things are."

"Just let it be; don't rock the boat."

Have you heard your inner voice make similar statements?

Take time right now to identify some of your own limiting thoughts.

*We cannot ✳
become what
we need to be
by remaining
what we are.*

–Max DePree

IMPT. TO IDENTIFY WHERE THESE "LIMITING THOUGHTS" ORIGINATED . . .

OGILVY: "THE TYRANNY OF REASON"

※ *This is the highest wisdom that I own… freedom and life are earned by those alone who conquer them each day anew.*

—Goethe

Can you pinpoint where and when these thoughts originated? Try to get some insight into how they changed from subtle, erroneous suggestions to ingrained beliefs about yourself. From there see if you can dig even deeper and discover how they prevented you from doing what you wanted to do and being what you wanted to be.

The good news is that the mere identification of these thoughts diminishes their power over you. By moving them from the recesses of the subconscious mind to the conscious, you have issued a challenge to their validity. A provocative statement by David Ogilvy, the advertising genius, might help you in this part of our work together: "The majority of business-people are incapable of original thought because they are unable to escape the tyranny of reason."

The tyranny of reason rules more than business-people. This tyrant ruthlessly reigns over many lives, keeping its subjects chained to limited, inflexible thinking, and, as a result, stifling both creativity and possibility.

Take a moment to experience the tyranny of reason by doing the exercise on the next page (this exercise may be familiar to you; if so, try it again to make sure you have the answer and/or spend some time reflecting on its implications).

Directions: Without lifting your pencil from the paper, draw four straight, connected lines that will go through all nine dots but through each dot only once. If you have not succeeded after a couple of attempts, ask yourself what restrictions you have set up for yourself involving this problem.

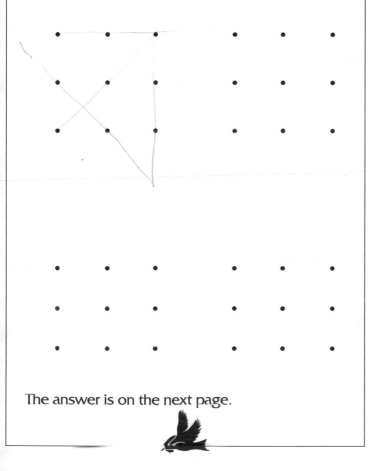

The answer is on the next page.

Men who are ✳
"orthodox"
when they
are young are
in danger
of being
middle-aged
all their lives.

–Walter Lippman

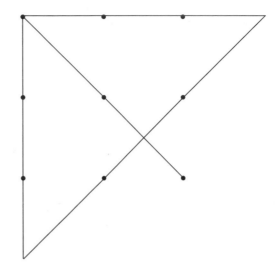

Most people assume a mental perimeter around the nine dots, thereby limiting any possible solution to the areas within the dots. By doing so, they limit themselves to within walls of their own creation. But the answer—and your future—lies outside those confines. To break through, however, will require nothing less than a coup d'etat, a mental revolution, to unseat the tyranny of those thoughts that continue to limit and rule your life.

A MENTAL
COUP D'ETAT !

Whatever the origin of these limiting thoughts, your most powerful weapon against them is your willingness to clarify and envision what you truly want for your life. This is the place where many people stumble and experience a sense of frustration. Some even give up, for we have had little, if any, schooling in identifying that which is important and motivating to us.

It is critical, however, that you begin and persist in stimulating your imagination with pictures of what an exciting future would look like for you. Mentally escaping the boundaries of the nine dots is the first step in creating what you want physically.

Let's assume, for example, that you could have anything you wanted. What would you choose? If the choices were unlimited, what would yours be? If anything were possible, what would you decide upon? Observe the way your mind talks to you about these questions. Does it resist or protest?

Your most powerful weapon against limiting thoughts is your willingness to clarify and envision what you truly want for your life.

Now, ignoring what you might feel is or is not possible or reasonable, write down at least five things you feel you really want.

The trouble with most people is that they think with their hopes or fears or wishes rather than with their minds.

–Will Durant

Take another look at what you have chosen. Do you desire the fruits of these choices enough that you would be willing to declare boldly (but privately) that these are the conditions, circumstances, and beliefs that you wish to see manifested in your life? This statement of what you want is called a positive affirmation.

The limiting thoughts you listed, when expressed verbally, are negative affirmations. You are an excellent witness to their power. This power exists because the language we use both reflect and affect our thinking. Mark Hopkins stated, "Language is the picture and counterpart of thought." That is why, if your future is not to be a mere repetition of your past, transforming your language to reflect what you want—not what you don't want—is a powerful tool to help you shape your thoughts.

Understand, however, that affirmations are just one tool and, by themselves, will not change your life. Without follow-up action, an affirmation is only an exercise in delusion. But as the lens is to a camera, an affirmation is a valuable mechanism for bringing into focus the scenes and events we wish to see recorded in our lives. A clear vision is the genesis of creation.

Let me suggest a beginning affirmation that has been of significant help to me in clearing away the cobwebs of my own limitations.

Transforming your language to reflect what you want is a powerful tool to help you shape your thoughts.

"I accept, I acknowledge only those thoughts that con-tribute to my success."

When making this declaration or any other affir-mation, put feeling into it. Actions trigger feelings just as feelings trigger actions. If you feel somewhat uncomfortable to begin with and are skeptical, that's quite normal. Affirmations could appear to be a sim-plistic approach to a deeply rooted, complex prob-lem, especially if you regard yourself as a sophisticat-ed and rational human being.

I have found, however, this affirmation to be most helpful, especially when self-doubt threatens to over-power me.

Once again, an affirmation is not a magic wand, but when you declare boldly and honestly what it is you want, this primary action mobilizes the thoughts and subsequent actions necessary for you to secure the object of your desire. But if affirmations still require a leap of faith, then take it, for <u>you won't dis-cover your wings until you leave the nest of your "reasonable" thoughts and behaviors.</u>

The journey upon which you are embarking will be an exciting and challenging one, and you cannot afford to carry with you any excess baggage of erro-neous beliefs. At every opportunity, expose them, examine them, own them, and finally discard them. As these mental roadblocks are gradually removed, what is possible for your life expands. You will begin to understand that you have the power to choose how you want to live, what you want to do, and who you wish to be. You can then envision a future that will inspire the dedication and commitment required to make what you dream come true.

The reasonable man adapts himself to the world: The unreasonable man persists in trying to adapt the world to himself. Therefore all progress depends on the unreasonable man.

–George Bernard Shaw

THE FREEDOM TO BE YOU

THE TRUE AMERICAN DREAM

CHAPTER 2

A national business paper, read by hundreds of thousands, advertises itself as the "Daily Diary of The American Dream." It is one highly visible example of how the definition of the American Dream has become so narrowly focused and misinterpreted.

The vision of those who, in 1776, declared the United States a sovereign nation is clearly described in the Declaration of Independence: "All men are created equal; . . . they are endowed by their creator with certain inalienable rights; . . . among these are life, liberty and the pursuit of happiness."

These moving words reach out to the most primary desire and motivation within each of us: the freedom to express ourselves fully and completely in whatever way we may choose. Because of unwavering commitment to these ideals, America became, and remains, a dynamic land, full of opportunity for those who have little chance of this freedom in their homelands.

The American Dream might therefore be more accurately described as the right and freedom to be who we want to be, and do exactly what we want to do, providing it does not infringe on the rights of others.

This understanding of the real promise of the American Dream is a cornerstone of learning to soar. The freedom to be who you want to be reinforces the

Ours is the only country founded on a good idea.

—John Gunther

philosophy that permeates these pages: "Above all, to thine own self be true." The most significant challenge life presents us with, however, is how can we be true to ourselves?

To begin with, you must be truthful in defining what it is you want for your life. You must assess what success means to you.

Consider the following questions:

Whom do you know who is successful?

Why would you regard them so?

How would you describe success?

What feelings would you associate with success?

What are you willing to do to achieve this success?

What are you not willing to do?

For journal entry

We live in a culture where winning is important. The sports pages are devoured daily. We exult in victory and are sad in defeat. Everybody is supposed to love a winner.

A sporting event, kept in perspective, is a minor aspect of life. Only the diehard enthusiast remembers the Super Bowl champion of ten years ago, let alone the gold medal winners of even the most recent Olympic Games. In many instances it is only the relatives and friends of those who came in second and third that recall their achievements.

You and I participate daily in a much more important event than can ever be found in the sports pages. If life is a school, is it not also a game, one that we all play but perhaps with little understanding of how to determine the score? How do we know whether we are winning the game of life? What is it that determines us to be winners? By what criteria do we judge our performance?

The dictionary defines *success* as a favorable result, wished-for ending. Most people describe happiness as the ultimate wished-for ending. Happiness, unlike a sporting event, is not a goal that we can take aim at and achieve. It results from the daily choices and decisions we make in our lives. One of those choices is to do something worthwhile and satisfying. Others involve the means we select to achieve our ends.

Because happiness is also defined individually by each of us, perhaps the only true means to judge success is this: being involved with and accomplishing that which results in the feelings we want to experience most of the time. Or put in another way: if because of who you are and/or what you do, you are a willing and committed participant in life, then you are successful—you are a winner.

In other words, success and winning are not measured by what you have or don't have. You can be rich and happy or rich and miserable. You can be poor and happy or poor and miserable. Winning is assessed simply by how you *feel* about life, and how you feel about life is determined by what your life is about.

It's pretty hard to find what does bring happiness. Poverty and wealth have both failed.

–Kin Hubbard

To understand this more fully we must examine a key characteristic of successful (i.e., happy and fulfilled) people: They love what they do because what they do is an expression of their gifts and talents.

When considering what it is you want the future to hold for you, it may be necessary to shift your thinking to a whole new level: understanding the distinction between career and vocation. Career is goal oriented, but vocation focuses on the purpose for your life.

Vocation originates in the Latin *vocare* meaning *to call*. Your vocation calls you to contribute your talents to work you love and believe in. Your career is, of course, important, but your vocation should guide and influence your choices of career. Career success is almost guaranteed to those who apply their gifts and talents to work they are passionate about.

To put career ahead of vocation points to being primarily concerned with upward mobility, advancement, and progress. This can lead to maneuvers that on the surface appear clever and smart, but often are manipulative, lack integrity, and inevitably come back to haunt you.

To be true to ourselves a career should be planned within the context of our vocation or calling. In no way does this limit us. Choosing to focus our talents toward what we truly love and believe in brings forth the creativity, energy, and commitment

Career is goal oriented, but vocation focuses on the purpose for your life.

that are key characteristics of any successful career. You will discover that your career goals are much more readily achieved when you are working *on purpose.*

I read recently in *Soundings,* a publication of The Economics Press, something that spoke to what I mean:

Make enjoyment of your work and your life your highest priority, rather than money. Not that the desire to be rich is bad. Almost everyone would enjoy being wealthy. The desire for luxuries is healthy and normal. Time and time again, however, studies have shown that people who make satisfaction in their work a top priority are the ones who perform best, receive the fastest promotions, and wind up making the most money. Those who make money their primary goal rarely achieve their economic goals and often wind up chronically unhappy.

If you are stuck in a job that you don't enjoy, you are unlikely to go very far in it even if you are being paid well. Money is simply not enough as a motivator. Maximum performance comes from maximum enjoyment.

If you make enjoyment of your work and your life a top priority, you will do your best, and very often that will be better than you think you can do. The result will be success, and money follows success just as naturally as morning follows dawn.

Although goals are certainly important markers on your journey through life, I believe that you and I were created for a reason that transcends the accomplishment of any goal. There is a purpose for our lives far grander and more significant than perhaps we might ever have considered.

The source of my own understanding and aware-ness in this area was the second major wake up call I experienced in my life. It revealed clearly to me the important distinction between vocation and career and, as a result, between purpose and goals. It began at a point when I was suffering from what might be termed *malnutrition of the soul.*

Having recovered from my financial disaster, I had once again achieved a very comfortable life. My career was accelerating and I had decided to accept an appointment as a senior executive with the inter-national consulting firm that I had been representing in the South Pacific. This necessitated moving to the United States.

Despite having once again acquired the trappings of success, I became strangely unsettled. This puz-zled me because conventional opinion would sug-gest that I should have been a turned-on, happy guy. I wasn't really unhappy; it was just that something was not quite as it should or could be.

Henry David Thoreau wrote, "The mass of men lead lives of quiet desperation." The key word for me was *quiet.* Although I would not acknowledge being desperate, I was thinking quietly: Is this all there is? Surrounded by the things we believe will bring us

There is a purpose for our lives far grander and more significant than perhaps we might ever have considered.

happiness, many of us are unwilling to admit that life is not meeting our expectations.

It was during a team building seminar that I was attending that I discovered a clue to my dilemma. The first question we were to answer seemed simple: What is the purpose of this team? Or put another way: Why does the team exist? I was amazed at how we struggled for agreement. It seemed that these questions were so rarely asked and thought about.

These questions brought to my mind others. What is the purpose of my life? Why do I exist? Why am I here? Intuitively, I knew that these were the questions to which I desperately needed answers. I hoped I could then determine what was missing in my life.

Success had always been my primary focus and, as I have mentioned, I had defined success as getting rich. I now slowly began to understand that it was not really money I was after but rather the things money could buy. These thoughts evolved into a profound realization that even things were not my main objective. What I had really wanted was *the feelings of success* that I believed things would bring. I looked at all the things I had accumulated and realized that this success did not feel as good as I believed it should. Suddenly another blinding glimpse of the obvious: *Things don't have feelings.* But if life was not about getting rich, then what else was there?

I have found that it is much easier to make a success in life than to make a success of one's life.

—G. W. Follin

Six months passed, satisfying answers still eluded me, and I drifted into a mild depression. One morning, too restless to sleep, I arose at 5 o'clock and made a cup of tea. Noticing a brown paper bag on the dresser, I remembered it contained a book purchased two weeks prior on a business trip to Canada. Resigned to having nothing better to do, I sat down and started to read the book. Two hours later, I surfaced exhilarated; I had broken through. The answers I had been seeking were cascading into place.

The book was a pictorial essay about the accomplishments of Terry Fox, a young Canadian who had completed the greatest marathon run in history. Averaging a marathon a day for five months, he ran 3,339 miles across Canada. The amazing thing is that Terry Fox was an amputee, a victim of cancer. He was running to raise money for cancer research when additional cancer was discovered in his lungs, and he was forced to give up short of his goal of crossing the entire width of Canada.

Why did he do it? His convalescence provides an important clue. Terry was devastated by what he witnessed in the hospital. Previously, he was quite ignorant of the insidiousness of cancer, but now he was shocked by what he saw and he was angry.

His anger was not at his own misfortune. It was directed at this disease that ravaged people's bodies and caused so much pain and suffering. So strong were these feelings that he decided that without a doubt, if he survived, one day he would join the fight to eliminate cancer. In the midst of adversity, at a time when others in similar circumstances would understandably be full of self-pity, Terry Fox discovered a purpose, a compelling reason to live. What had now been revealed, he felt, was much more important and urgent than his own difficulties.

As Terry's story sank in, I contemplated and wondered at the implications of being committed to something that transcended oneself. I began to experience a dramatic shift in my perspective as I saw so clearly the futility of living life purely for oneself. The void I felt was impossible to fill with things. I recalled my disappointment at the many times I had reached a goal, only to discover that the good feelings were temporary and fleeting.

That missing something, the emptiness I had been experiencing, was clearly caused by a lack of purpose, the absence of any compelling reason to live. I continued to make connections as it came to me that the overall purpose of my life was no different from Terry's. Of course, that's why I exist: to contribute, to serve, to reach beyond myself and make a difference in this world. But was that not true for all of us? Isn't that why there are no two people alike, so that all of us can be of service in our own special way? Are we merely freaks of nature, or is there something different and valuable in each individual that only he or she can contribute to the world?

The depth of feelings that accompanied these insights was amazing. I could never ever recall being so moved, so inspired. The experience had a very special quality to it, a wholeness, an integrity. I felt an incredible sense of power, one quite different from the driving motivation I had felt before. There are times when intuitively you know something is right, and this was one of those times.

It was becoming clear to me that the only purpose worthy of humankind was to make the world a better place in which to live. Was that not the motivation for civilization itself? I began to understand that, unquestionably, my life was important, that whatever I could contribute was both necessary and needed. Even though there were five billion inhabitants of this planet, I knew my life mattered.

Albert Einstein implied that the only reason he found for human existence is that man is here for the sake of other men only.

There are many people who, for various reasons, would ridicule these conclusions and who would think it is too big a leap of faith to really believe that, in the bigger picture, each of us counts. But for me it was not a difficult decision. My heart said yes and my mind agreed, and I learned long ago that when heart and mind are in harmony, tune in to that melody.

Nothing is so intolerable to man as being fully at rest, without a passion, without business, without entertainment, without care.

–Blaise Pascal

Terry Fox's accomplishments were quite astounding: an average athlete, who completed one of the greatest marathons in history; a shy introvert who gave passionate speeches to thousands of people; a lonely runner who captured the imagination of a nation and became their hero—all this seemed to be traceable back to the commitment to, and strength of, his purpose.

Dr. Charles Garfield, author of *Peak Performers,* says, "Peak performers are people who are committed to a compelling mission. It is very clear that they care deeply about what they do and their efforts, energies and enthusiasms are traceable back to that particular mission."

Most of us are perhaps not destined to match the efforts of Terry Fox, but still the lesson is there. Gail Sheehy, in her best seller, *Pathfinders,* writes, "My research offers impressive evidence that we feel better when we attempt to make our world better . . . to have a purpose beyond one's self lends to existence a meaning and direction—the most important characteristic of high well-being."

Since discovering Terry Fox's story, I have become aware of the commonality of people in terms of what most of us really want. Security, prosperity, fulfillment, love, peace, and harmony are on the list of goals for many of us. Like happiness, however, they are not really goals but the result of choice, a commitment to a way of life.

Martin Mull, actor and comedian, who wrote *The History of White People in America,* was asked by a television interviewer to describe one chapter that deals with the soul of a white person. "First of all, it's important to understand they are a contradiction in terms," he responded. Mull's humor drives home to me how good a job many of us, of all colors, have done denying the existence of our souls. But until we ✳ make the decision to not sell our souls pursuing our careers, true success will elude us.

This takes us back to why this chapter was subtitled "The True American Dream." If the primary responsibility we have in life is being true to ourselves, it can only be accomplished by carrying out what we are called to do—our unique and special vocation. The True American Dream not only provides the freedom to use our gifts and talents to achieve our highest goals, but also the freedom to fulfill our purpose in life. While goals nourish the heart, it is purpose that feeds the soul.

An unknown author gave the following perspective on life. Read it slowly and check out your response to each statement:

> *Do not commit the error, common among the young, of assuming that if you cannot save the whole of mankind you have failed.*
>
> –Jan de Hartog

What is Life?

Life is a gift . . . accept it

Life is an adventure . . . dare it

Life is a mystery . . . unfold it

Life is a game . . . play it

Life is struggle . . . face it

Life is beauty . . . praise it

Life is a puzzle . . . solve it

Life is opportunity . . . take it

Life is sorrowful . . . experience it

Life is a song . . . sing it

Life is a goal . . . achieve it

Life is a mission . . . fulfill it

This is truly a philosophy that can make life work. It is a wisdom that can lead to being both healthy and wealthy. It is a foundation upon which you can build not only worldly success, but also have that which is beyond fame or fortune: a peaceful soul.

As you learn to soar, understand that those whose vocation directs them toward a successful business career are to be supported and encouraged. Equally deserving of support and encouragement, however, are those who, in being true to themselves, choose a path where the rewards are less visible but whose contributions are no less significant in terms of their enrichment of our society.

> *Unless there be correct thought, there cannot be any action, and when there is correct thought, right action will follow.*
>
> –Henry George

Why You Are Here

The Power of Purpose

Chapter
3

How you live your life and what you do with it shapes not only your own future but that of the world. In this chapter we shall explore your importance to this planet.

Our world has been profoundly influenced by the thoughts, beliefs, and actions of all its past and present inhabitants. History is created not only by those whose names are revered and celebrated, but also by the infamous and unknown. All who have lived have carved, in some way, their own special niche.

In his book, The Star Thrower, *Loren E. Eiseley talks of the day when he was walking along a sandy beach where thousands of starfish had been washed up on the shore. He noticed a boy picking up the starfish one by one and throwing them back into the ocean. Eiseley observed the boy for a few minutes and then asked what he was doing. The boy replied that he was returning the starfish to the sea otherwise they would die.*

Eiseley then asked how saving a few, when so many were doomed, would make any difference whatsoever? The boy picked up a starfish and as he threw it back said, "It's going to make a lot of difference to this one."

Eiseley left the boy and went home to continue writing, only to find he could not type a single word. He returned to the beach and spent the rest of the day helping the boy throw starfish into the sea.

Robert Kennedy and Loren Eiseley suggest that it doesn't matter whether or not as individuals we rank among the famous. What does matter is that each of

> *Few will have the greatness to bend history itself, but each of us can work to change a small portion of events. . . . It is from numberless acts of courage and belief that human history is shaped.*
>
> —Robert F. Kennedy

us has a purpose in life—to somehow make a positive contribution to the world in which we live.

With five billion inhabitants already on planet
Earth, however, it can be "reasonably" difficult to
believe that there could be a special purpose for each
and every one of our lives. It is easy to feel insignifi-
cant among the multitudes.

But nothing will have a more positive effect on
your level of accomplishment, fulfillment, and happiness than the belief and understanding that you do
bring to humanity something special that no one else
can offer. The most important thought that you can
ever hold is: Your life matters.

During the writing of this book, I hit several creative blocks. Even when I was bursting to express
ideas, sometimes the words on the paper seemed to
fall short of conveying the passion I felt for the subject. Self-doubt surfaced and the vision that my work
would bear fruit was severely dimmed.

I soon learned, however, that when a project is
worthy and there is strong commitment to its com-
pletion, a phenomenon comes into play known as "a
meaningful coincidence." It functions as encouragement to persist and not give up. In a later chapter this
phenomenon is more fully discussed, but I want to
mention one such incident because it is appropriate
here.

Our family was on summer vacation at a peaceful,

sheltered cabin in Wisconsin. One morning, as I sat on the back deck struggling to write, an elderly gentleman approached. He was very friendly, and we struck up quite a conversation. He had retired, he told me, but had taken on a part-time job tending the grounds around our cabin and the surrounding area.

His parting words helped me understand how our meeting had been a meaningful coincidence. Explaining why he continued to work, he said, "You know, I'd go crazy if I weren't being useful." The insight stimulated by my new friend's words reinforced for me why my efforts were worthwhile.

Life is empty if we are not useful. We defy a primary purpose of our existence when we are not being useful. We abandon our gifts and talents and destroy the creative force within us when we are not being useful. We sacrifice joy, happiness, fulfillment, peace, and contentment when we are not being useful.

We were born, I believe, to be "thoroughly used up" when we die. That is not to say that we exhaust ourselves, frantically filling our days with meaningless activities. Rather, it means understanding that we were created to fulfill a purpose and it is that purpose that empowers, inspires, and gives meaning to our lives.

Consider those people who have earned the modern world's respect: Mother Teresa, Walt Disney,

Lech Walesa, Lee Iacocca, Mikhail Gorbachev, Nelson Mandela, and so many others. They have significantly different beliefs, callings, and careers, but their commonality is that each has *the power of purpose* in their lives.

There are many more people, however, who are relatively unknown, but who share with these honored and admired figures a deep sense of purpose. They are homemakers, artists, businesspeople, school teachers, and volunteers; you will find them in every walk of life. Their common, priceless legacy is that because of them the world is a better place.

Bob Doss began the Upward Bound Academy, located in Bridgeport, Connecticut, after his daughter began to speak of the many kids she knew who were dropping out of high school. Remembering his own struggles in school and college, he felt a tremendous desire to take charge and "do something." Bob Doss saw an urgent need to give these going-nowhere kids a chance in life.

The academy was founded in 1986 with $25,000 of Bob's own money for a clear purpose: to get inner-city girls into college. Using a unique blend of athletics and academics, the academy has already not only earned a reputation as a basketball powerhouse, but also is getting kids into college who would not ordinarily make it. If you have not heard of Bob Doss it does not matter, he has the power of purpose.

The antithesis of having a purpose is the empty life where there is no meaning, where the daily

The great and glorious masterpiece of man is how to live with purpose.

–Michel de Montaigne

objective is simply survival. This is the life that continually needs to be filled up from the outside and where the lack of purpose is often manifested physically in apathy, disease, drugs, alcohol abuse, and suicide.

In his best-selling book, *Love, Medicine & Miracles*, Dr. Bernie Siegel says of his breakthrough work in healing cancer patients, "One of the most common precursors of cancer is . . . a feeling of emptiness in one's life."

For what purpose were you created?

In the final analysis, this is a question that only you can answer; no one else can give you a sense of purpose. But understand that it is a sense. More than a rational conclusion, it is instinctive and intuitive. The answer to whether there is a purpose for your life requires searching beyond your mind into your heart and soul.

The impersonal hand of government can never replace the helping hand of a neighbor.

–Hubert H. Humphrey

As I have revealed in earlier chapters, I have been down many paths looking for happiness. My reading has been prolific as I have searched for a meaning for my life. But nothing has made more sense and has subsequently resulted in more peace, contentment, and fulfillment than this understanding:

The purpose of life is to be a growing, contributing human being.

Life is at its very best when people are willingly and happily contributing to each other. We love to go to a place of worship where the celebrant is inspiring. We love to be with friends who accept, encourage, and listen to us. We love to shop in stores where we feel welcome and important. We love to go to concerts where the music lifts our spirits and moves our souls.

Clearly, what distinguishes truly successful people is that they are contributors. They are in love with life and all the possibilities of what it means to be human. Their accomplishments, their successes, are rooted in their desire to grow and be of service to humanity.

The idea of service and contribution is not new, but to many people the idea of serving connotes an inferior status. Those famous contributors and servers already mentioned, however, do not feel and certainly are not regarded as inferior. Perhaps that is because they understand what Victor Frankl suggested, "One need not be a servant to be able to serve."

Each of us will define and measure success differently. Some will place more emphasis on the economic scorecard than others. No matter what your choice, if you are to succeed, you must understand that your rewards in life will be in direct proportion to the contribution you make.

Grasp fully this fundamental principle, apply it to your work, and you will have little concern over money again. Apply it to your personal and professional relationships, and you will be overwhelmed

The purpose of life is to be a growing, contributing human being.

with the love, admiration, and respect you receive from others.

On a business trip to Nashville I had my shoes shined for the first time by someone other than myself. Zee was a master craftsman. Not only did he treat my shoes as if they were the finest pair he had ever seen, but his interest in me as a person had me believing I was the most fascinating individual he had ever met. Zee's enthusiasm was infectious, and he was reward-ed with a line six deep waiting for his services. In reply to a question about his work, he said, "No, sir, I'm happy here; I love what I'm doing and I make good money."

I thought to myself, "This guy has it all—love, happiness, and money—and yet he shines shoes." Once again, I learned that what we do is not as important as how and why we do it. Zee was happy to be "of service," yet he was not at all sub-servient; in fact, he was a model of dignity. I also noticed that he was making good money. That positive, attentive attitude was paying off with some excellent tips.

Your rewards in life will be in direct proportion to the contribution you make.

I walked away from Zee reflecting on how he had so masterfully applied the principle of contribution to create a modest but successful business. He had much to teach many of the larger and more sophisti-cated enterprises whose competitive difficulties in recent years could clearly be traced back to having lost sight of their primary purpose. If you have made your career in the business world, it is a most worth-while exercise to examine how contribution is the key ingredient of the purpose of a business.

The average person, when asked, "What is the purpose of a business?" answers, "To make a profit."

Over the past two decades the philosophy that the bottom line is the primary reason for the existence of a business has brought considerable grief to many organizations. Profits declined and losses mounted as competitors carved bigger and bigger slices out of their market share. Desperate to find answers, their most startling revelation has been that they lost sight of their true purpose, that which had made their businesses successful and viable enterprises in the first place.

Theodore Leavitt, professor of marketing at Harvard University, states simply and directly in his book, *The Marketing Imagination,* "The purpose of a business is to create and keep a customer."

A business opportunity occurs when there is a problem to be solved or a need to be met. The entrepreneur seizes the opportunity and produces a product or service that will solve the problem or meet the need. The key ingredient to the success of the business, however, is the ability to attract and retain customers. Without customers, absolutely nothing else is possible, nothing else matters. When management takes its eye off this business ball, the seeds of trouble are sown. That ball is its fundamental reason for being—its purpose.

Profit is not the purpose of a business. Profit is a

Money never starts an idea; it is the idea that starts the money.

–W.J. Cameron

dynamic incentive and motivator for being in business. In order to sustain the business—for it to grow and remain healthy—profits are obviously essential. But distinguishing the role of profits from the purpose of the business is vital to understanding how consistent, long-term profits are best achieved.

Profit is both the result and reward of doing things right and doing the right things. The ability to attract customers, withstand competition, and implement sound management practices, all carefully blended together, create a successful business. Doing things right and doing the right thing, however, also makes a statement about the culture of a business.

Leavitt is most emphatic when he stresses the importance of clarifying the purpose of a business. "For people of affairs, a statement of purpose should provide guidance to the management of their affairs. To say that they should attract and hold customers, forces facing the necessity of figuring out what people really want and value, and then catering to those wants and values. It provides special guidance and has moral merit."

Profit is both the result and reward of doing things right and doing the right things.

This is to say that profits are well-deserved and justified when a business sees as its primary reason for existing to contribute to the well-being of its customers. Or, in other words, well-served and satisfied customers build profitable, lasting businesses.

Consider now the universe itself and how things

work in the cosmos. Do you spend much time star-
gazing? On a clear night, with the air crisp and clean,
looking at the stars and the magnificence of the universe, one is filled with awe. At first, only the brighter,
more obvious stars get our attention. But gradually
the distant twinkling of thousands of others comes
into focus, and as our vision expands so do our
thoughts, until the entire scene of millions of planets
is exhilarating.

The Earth reminded us of a Christmas tree ornament hang-
ing in the blackness of space. As we got farther and farther away
It diminished in size. Finally it shrank to the size of a marble, the
most beautiful marble you can imagine. That beautiful, warm,
living object looked so fragile, so delicate, that if you touched it
with a finger it would crumble and fall apart. Seeing this has to
change a man, has to make a man appreciate the creation of
God and the love of God.

–James Irwin, Astronaut

Basic science teaches us how the sun and moon
contribute to the earth. Without the sun, life would
not be possible. It provides the vital energy necessary
for growth. The moon with its gravitational pull con-
trols our tides. On earth, nature is continually performing an intricate balancing act in order to sustain
life. Is it not amazing that everything stays so order-
ly? Scientists tell us it is all the components of the
universe working together in a form of massive cooperation. Probe further and you will discover that the

principle of contribution is actually woven into the very fabric of the universe.

One morning I woke up and decided to look out the window, to see where we were. We were flying over America and suddenly I saw snow, the first snow we ever saw from orbit. Light and powdery, it blended with the contours of the land, with the veins of the rivers. I thought autumn, snow—people are busy getting ready for winter. A few minutes later we were flying over the Atlantic, then Europe, and then Russia. I have never visited America, but I imagined that the arrival of autumn and winter is the same there as in other places, and the process of getting ready for them is the same. And then it struck me that we are all children of our Earth. It does not matter what country you look at. We are all Earth's children, and we should treat her as our Mother.

—Aleksandr Aleksandrov, Cosmonaut

In some sense man is a microcosm of the universe; therefore what man is, is a clue to the universe; we are enfolded in the universe.

—David Bohm

The social philosopher Marshall McLuhan suggested that on spaceship earth there are no passengers, only crew. To accept our status as crew means to accept responsibility for what happens to our world. Is there a more worthy purpose?

As crew members, each of us must choose an assignment. Some of us will lead, others will follow. At no time, however, should we make the mistake of comparing, underestimating or overestimating, devaluing or overvaluing, the worthiness of what we do. Each contribution is of vital importance when it helps to steer the world in the direction we want it to go.

Time magazine could not have been more passionate in its plea for this level of responsibility than when it discarded its traditional Person of the Year, in 1988, to name Earth Planet of the Year. Thomas A. Sanction, in the lead article, wrote, "Man has reached a point in his evolution where he has the power to affect, for better or worse, the present and future state of the planet. . . . He finds himself at a crucial turning point, the actions of those now living will determine the future, and possibly the very survival, of the species. . . . Now, more than ever, the world needs leaders who can inspire their fellow citizens with a fiery sense of mission."

In *Illusions,* the writer Richard Bach says, "He teaches that which he most needs to learn." I believe our bond lies in a common desire to discover a purpose worthy of our deepest commitment.

Solomon, when given a blank check by God to choose whatever he wanted for his life, chose wisdom. Here, then, is a distillation of the wisdom of the philosophers, spiritual teachers, psychologists, and psychiatrists who throughout history have sought the prescription for a happy life.

Each night before you go to sleep, ask yourself two simple questions:

Did I today, in someway, grow as a human being?

Did I today, in anyway, make the world a better place in which to live?

> *Sometimes I think we're alone in the universe, and sometimes I think we're not. In either case, the idea is quite staggering.*
>
> —Arthur C. Clarke

When you can answer yes to these questions more often than not, you are winning—you are successful.

Having a purpose for one's life is not a panacea for happiness or perpetual good feelings. It is, however, the fundamental answer to what makes living worthwhile, no matter how grave the challenges. As Nietzsche wrote, "He who has a *why* to live can bear almost any *how*."

The power of purpose can certainly bring you fame and fortune. The real treasure, however, lies much more in how it enriches your life. The power of your purpose will help you access the only power that really matters: the confidence to move forward, to risk, to live the life you imagine for yourself with the security, that no matter the obstacles along the way, you know you can handle them. It is a power that emanates from the deepest part of you, and there is not a human being alive within whom this power does not exist.

How shall the soul of a man be larger than the life he has lived?

–Edgar Lee Masters

THE QUEST FOR DIGNITY

SELF-APPRECIATION

CHAPTER
4

Our efforts so far have focused on that which inspires and gives impetus to our lives and, in the final analysis, what makes life worthwhile. There is now a final, critical project we must undertake before we can begin the design phase of learning to soar. It is to discover your true heritage as a member of the human family. Only when this process is complete can you begin to fully open up, to imagine all that is possible for your life.

I have chosen to use self-appreciation to describe this part of our work together because it means "to value oneself highly." Self-appreciation leads to healthy self-esteem, a positive self-image, and a feeling of being worthy, but it also leads to the most important result of this level of understanding: a sense of dignity, a complete and absolute respect for oneself.

When Mother Teresa began her work, she stated that her mission was to have those to whom she ministered live the last moments of their lives with dignity. Through loving and caring, she sought to bring them to an understanding that, no matter how different and difficult their lives had been, they were still, in her words, children of God. For Mother Teresa, it is never, ever too late to discover who we are. And for us, it is essential to be connected to the source of our existence.

Whatever this work requires of you, be willing to

The true self is always in motion like music, a river of life, changing, moving, failing, suffering, learning, shining.

–Brenda Ueland

undertake it. The quality of your life will directly
reflect your commitment to this process, for self-
appreciation is the foundation upon which your future
should be built.

Have you ever seen a boat in dry dock? It is the
place where the boat is lifted from the water for the
purpose of repairing and cleaning the hull. Over time,
various forms of debris accumulate on the hull, which
has the effect of slowing the boat down because of
increased resistance in the water. A well-maintained
and clean hull minimizes this resistance and enables
the boat to maximize its capabilities.

No matter what your age, the essence of who
you are has been covered up over the years by layers
of beliefs and assumptions about yourself and others.
These began accumulating from the time you were
born and resulted from the interactions with the people and tasks in your life. From what transpired in
these interactions, you came to conclusions about
yourself and your place in the world. Many of these
conclusions were incorrect because they were based
on erroneous information. They are true for you only
because you *believe* them to be so.

This is not to suggest that all we know about ourselves is invalid. We can all identify valuable lessons
and insights into ourselves from which we have benefited. For far too many of us, however, the challenges of the years have meant the accumulation of

limiting beliefs and assumptions that blur our vision of what is possible for our lives. Our task now is to accelerate the work we began in chapter 1 and identify more of those false, spirit-destroying messages that you have accepted as truth over the years. The goal is to reveal a person worthy of actually having whatever it is you desire for your life.

Full self-appreciation requires both a willingness to enter a mental dry dock and a commitment to remove the debris that has accumulated on the hull of your life. This debris is primarily the false beliefs and assumptions about yourself resulting from past mistakes and failures. They now handicap your every move. Until this repair and cleaning work is undertaken, unnecessary resistance will hold you back from using your full potential.

I experienced the benefits of the dry dock process following the third and most ruthless of my wake-up calls.

After many years of clearly being second in priority to my often thoughtless and inconsiderate work habits, plus the innocent victim of other unacceptable behaviors on my part, my wife decided to separate from me. With our five children, she returned to Australia. The marriage made in heaven had gone to hell.

I was left stunned by the shocking realization that what I truly loved—my family—had walked out of my life. I became paralyzed, not physically, but men-

tally. I was unable in many ways to function effectively. My work seemed empty and meaningless. My
motivation dropped to zero.

There are many self-destructive ways that, in
times like these, people try to console themselves. I
cannot recall why (perhaps it was lessons learned
from my previous wake-up calls), but in my desperation, I reached out for help and solace from friends.
My feelings of guilt, however, left little doubt that I
was worthy only of rejection, for no treatment would
be too harsh for my transgressions. Instead, to my
relief, those in whom I confided responded with
understanding and love. The more I unburdened my
soul, the more their compassion and support grew. I
then became confused. You have to be good to be
loved was the message of my childhood and yet
here I was, a mature man, admitting to being "bad"
and on the receiving end of more real love than at
any time in my life! What was happening?

The puzzle, after much discussion and reflection,
was eventually solved by my becoming aware that
real love was a stranger to me. I had lived under the
delusion that love was a reward for the things I did.
This was the result of receiving a considerable
amount of conditional love (praise for specific behaviors) during my early years. Conditional love is not
love at all, I discovered, but merely approval for
meeting someone else's standards.

A marriage without conflicts is almost as inconceivable as a nation without crises.

—André Maurois

The love that I was now receiving had no conditions attached to it. It was offered freely and seemed to give great pleasure to the giver. Nothing was being asked of me in return, and the more I opened up, the more this love poured in.

What I did not realize was how much the sharing of my struggles was helping those who listened to them. They, too, had made mistakes, many of which they had been unwilling to confront, but now my revelations gave them the courage to do so. Together we discovered that our failings were part of the human condition and that the primary challenge of life itself was to transcend and learn from these errors in order to live a richer and more effective life. Little did I know, however, that the door to my future would finally be thrust open by an experience so powerful that it would remove most of the guilt, debris, and emotional garbage that, over the years, had collected on the hull of my life.

As I came to fully appreciate how my friends truly loved and cared for me, I was led to reflect on the relationship I had with God. To that point, my thoughts had been only what a major disappointment I must be. But if God is love, as I believed, then perhaps, like my friends, there was a chance that I was still worthy of love. My past behavior, I thought, would require an awful lot of forgiveness on God's part.

Friend: one who knows all about you and loves you just the same.

—Elbert Hubbard

With a sense of blinding urgency, the word forgiveness began to flash like a neon sign in my mind.
An answer then followed, which remains to this day
the most important turning point in my life: *Love and
forgiveness are one.*

At no point had God stopped loving me, for since
God is unconditional love, God is also unconditional
forgiveness. Any pain I continued to experience was
not God's work but the result of my own unwilling-
ness to forgive and love myself.

This stream of fresh insights began to energetically disperse the dark clouds of negativity remaining in
my mind. I knew I had to accept the consequences of
my actions, but there was no value in mercilessly
dwelling on the events themselves. I knew I had to
be responsible and make amends, but I needed also
to move forward, taking with me once again the wisdom from my experience in order to improve the
integrity and quality of my future life.

It became clear that out of these lessons would
come much permanent and lasting good, but the
task of actually forgiving myself was still to be completed. I have since discovered that forgiveness of
self and others is one of the toughest challenges any
of us has to face. It requires surrender and humility,
two qualities not known as my strong points.

Ultimately I found a solution that made the forgiveness possible. Like so many other breakthroughs,

the solution was childlike in its simplicity. I reasoned: "If God is willing to forgive, then who am I to hold out?" With inexplicable relief, I finally let go of the tremendous burden that for so long had been stifling my life.

It is impossible to describe the wonderful sense of peace and serenity that immediately enfolded me. I knew that forgiveness was a most special gift, one I must carry into my new life and, wherever possible, share with others.

Subsequently, I have learned much about the power of forgiveness. It is now regarded by many therapists as an essential ingredient in healing not only emotional wounds, but also physical ailments. They suggest that high blood pressure, bad digestion, and loss of sleep, to name just a few, can be traced back to feelings of anger, resentment, and of being unfairly treated. With forgiveness, their patients, time after time, are restored to good health.

Dr. Bernie Siegel, in his well-documented, seemingly miraculous work with cancer patients, prescribes daily doses of forgiveness. He says emphatically, "You can learn to forgive yourself. You can't change your shortcomings until you accept yourself despite them."

Forgiveness is that with which we clean the hull of our lives. Resentment and anger toward others or ourselves from past mistakes, no matter how severe,

The heart's memory eliminates the bad and magnifies the good; and thanks to this artifice we manage to endure the burdens of the past.

–Gabriel García Márquez

are the debris that we must remove before we can successfully soar into a positive future.

Here are two inspiring examples:

Le Ly Hayslip is one who speaks of forgiveness as easily as she speaks of personal tragedy. During the Vietnam war soldiers tortured her by sending electric shocks through wires attached to her body. Then, tied to a stake in the hot afternoon sun, honey was poured on her feet to attract biting ants.

Despite these and other gross indignities, Le Ly has managed over twenty plus years to heal the physical and psychological wounds and has put her experiences into a book, When Heaven and Earth Changed Places.

The power of forgiveness has been such in her life that it has inspired a vision to "build a bridge between Vietnam and the United States . . . to heal the veterans and Vietnamese people."

In her words, "We must forgive every single human being in the whole world, not just Vietnam and the United States, but the whole planet. We're here together."

Stephen Budiansky, in a US News & World Report *article entitled, "An Antidote for the Legacy of Hatred," wrote the following about a remarkable man. "There is hope in South Africa, and it comes from the refusal of Nelson Mandela to make his own martyrdom—or the martyrdom of his people . . . the issue. After twenty-seven years in prison, he shows not a hint of bitterness toward his jailors, calling instead for dignity and understanding of the white minority's fears."*

It is time to enter your dry dock.

As you prepare to go through what I believe will

be one of the most challenging exercises of your life, let me offer support. There is nothing that has ever happened to you or anyone else that cannot be forgiven. We have all done things we would rather forget, but these unrecoverable actions can either leave us permanently handicapped or be an invaluable springboard of experience into the future.

Many people deny and try to forget their past because it is too painful to confront, especially if they regard their wrongdoing as a major offense. All of us, however, have a dark side, and if we are not to deceive ourselves, we must acknowledge the truth of its existence.

Let us begin the cleansing process. Write down any mistakes, failures, or things that you have done that you now know need to be forgiven. Include in the list the hurts and resentments you still hold toward others. There should be no boundaries or restrictions to what you acknowledge, since no one will see your list, unless you choose to share it. Remember, your past cannot be changed, but you can change tomorrow by your actions today!

Whatever emotions accompany this exercise, experience them fully, for they are a part of releasing the past. Of all the lessons I have learned over the years, one that has been immeasurably helpful is to validate my feelings and not make them wrong. When I do not resist my feelings of sadness, for

There is nothing that has ever happened to you or anyone else that cannot be forgiven.

example, I seem to pass through the sadness more quickly. Feelings are real, but unpredictable, so learn to understand and work with them.

Your past cannot be changed, but you can change tomorrow by your actions today.

I need to forgive myself for:

I need to forgive others for:

*Until you make
peace with
who you are,
you'll never be
content with
what you have.*

–Doris Mortman

When you have finished (there are no time limits), reflect upon the positive side of the past and what you have learned. Consider how, because of your experience, you are now a much more whole person. Think about what you can offer to the world because of what you now know. C. F. Kettering stated, "My interest is in the future, because I'm going to spend the rest of my life there."

Finally, the process must begin, to let go fully and completely and release the past. You may, of course, choose your own course of action, but here are some suggestions in the form of affirmations:

"I forgive and let go all the errors, mistakes, and failures of my life. The lessons have been well learned."

"I totally and unconditionally forgive myself and others for the errors, mistakes, and failures of the past. I am a wiser, more understanding human being."

Whatever words you choose, repeat them over and over until they ring with the truth. Realize there is so much for you to contribute and accomplish in the future that it serves no one for you to hold back and not bring to the world all that you have to offer.

Into the void that forgiveness creates rush many rewards. In my case, what struck me immediately was the profound sense of dignity, of being worthy of consideration, of self-respect. There is no doubt that this played a major role in the reconciliation between my wife and me, for it made possible honest communication, free of accusations and excuses. The separation lasted fifteen months and two very different people emerged, but the relationship, through forgiveness, now continually grows stronger.

Acceptance—coming to terms with your own humanness and being at peace with all your imperfections—is another wonderful reward of forgiveness. It is the understanding that your journey through life is special, that the twists and turns and detours have made you what you are today. Acceptance is the comfort that comes with the realization that paradoxically we are perfect, imperfect human beings.

The ultimate reward of forgiveness is love. Not narcissistic, it is a love of self and others born of surrender, thankfulness, and humility, an understanding love that recognizes the insecurity of all human beings. It is a love that also provides the courage to move confidently toward a better future. Finally, because it is unconditional and always present, this love breeds serenity and peace of mind.

Earlier in this chapter, I suggested that the goal of this process was to reveal a worthy and deserving human being capable of manifesting whatever you hold precious in your heart. It is my most heartfelt wish and hope that you have participated fully in this process of forgiveness and are already beginning to experience its rewards. If, like me, you have a belief in a Higher Power, I know you have made a strong

If you're going to do something tonight that you'll be sorry for tomorrow morning, sleep late.

–Henny Youngman

connection to the source of your being. Whatever your convictions I hope you understand the necessity of, and are succeeding in, releasing any burdens from the past.

After a while you learn the difference, subtle difference,
Between holding a hand and chaining a soul,

And you learn that love doesn't mean leaning
and company doesn't mean security,

And you begin to learn that kisses aren't contracts
and presents aren't promises,

And you begin to accept your defeats
with your head up and your eyes open,
with the grace of an adult, not the grief of a child,

And you learn to build all your roads on today
because tomorrow's ground is too uncertain for plans.

After a while you learn that even sunshine burns
if you get too much.

So plant your own garden and decorate your own soul,
instead of waiting for someone to bring you flowers

And you learn that you really can endure . . .
that you really are strong.

And that you really do have worth.

–Anonymous

You are now poised for the second task of self-appreciation, one that will be a cornerstone of your future. Simply because you are a human being, you bring much to the world. Add the richness of your life experiences, and suddenly you are wealthy—not necessarily in material terms, but in character and wisdom.

It is time to fully understand and appreciate the composition of this wealth, what you bring to life, to your relationships, to your work, and to anything else that has meaning for you. You have demonstrated the courage to deal with the regrets of the past; now you deserve to be acknowledged for all that is good and positive in your life.

You are a combination of the natural gifts and talents with which you were born, the knowledge you have acquired, and the skills you have developed. You are a friend, a lover, a spouse, or perhaps even all of them. You have a personality that has evolved and an intellect that has maturity. You are, in summary, an ordinary, miraculous member of the human family, but also different and special.

Take time now to become aware of how you are special, to do an inventory of everything that is you. There are minimal guidelines in this exercise, for it is most important that your mind have the opportunity to roam unrestricted into every aspect of who you are.

My assets are (qualities and characteristics you
regard as valuable):

Too many ✳
*people
overvalue
what they
are not and
undervalue
what they are.*

–Malcom Forbes

My talents are (natural abilities and aptitudes):

*Most human
beings have an
almost infinite
capacity for
taking things
for granted.*

–Aldous Huxley

My skills are (competencies acquired through practice):

My mother has always been unhappy with what I do. She would much rather I do something nicer, like be a bricklayer.

–Mick Jagger

My strengths are (distinguish the top two from each of the previous three categories):

Nobody's ever the greatest anything.

–Maralyn Lois Polak

As you move through this process, understand that any struggle is quite normal. Self-analysis, not a common occurrence for most of us, requires considerable thought and application. Focusing entirely on the positive can also add to the difficulty. This is not a time for false modesty, however, for you need to be aware of everything you have going for you as you create your future. At all times, I encourage you to add to the lists. With what you have been willing to do in this chapter alone, you deserve to feel good about yourself.

Take a final moment to reflect on our definition of self-appreciation: to value oneself highly. I hope you have already felt some movement toward a greater level of self-appreciation. No matter the immediate outcome, however, it is my promise to you that by revisiting the exercises in this chapter with sincerity and commitment, you will be rewarded with an ever-increasing respect and esteem for yourself.

There are parts of a boat which, taken by themselves, would sink. The engine would sink. The propeller would sink. But when the parts of a boat are built together, they float. So with the events of my life. Some have been tragic. Some have been happy. But when they are built together, they form a craft that floats and is going some place. And I am comforted.

With the foundation now laid and this cornerstone in place, it is time to discover your wings and learn how to soar in this changing world.

Live all you ✳ *can; it's a mistake not to. It doesn't so much matter what you do in particular, so long as you have your life. If you haven't had that, what have you had?*

–Henry James

CLARIFYING WHAT MATTERS MOST TO YOU

DEFINING YOUR MISSION

CHAPTER
5

Throughout the ages sages and philosophers have referred to a place within each of us called the higher self. This self, they suggest, persistently sends messages designed to protect our integrity, our wholeness as human beings. When listened to, our higher selves communicate what we value, what is important and matters most to us.

The world, however, is awash with misinformation that competes vigorously with and confuses these messages. "Defining Your Mission" is the process of tuning out this distortion and discovering what it is you truly want for your life.

Our allies in this endeavor will be the soul, the heart, and the creative mind. The soul is that which pulls us toward a meaningful purpose for our lives. The heart shows us our true feelings about where we want to go and what we want to do. The creative mind focuses on the big picture, thus helping us to rise above our fears and limitations.

In your life you will, I hope, be encouraged and supported by many people. Ultimately, though, it is a solo event. You must set the standards for your own success. You must not be misled by measurements that are not yours. Others may inspire and be role models for you, but finally you must trust your own sense of what is right for you.

The payoff for these efforts will be substantial. You will gain a new understanding and insight into why

There is no higher religion than human service. To work for the common good is the highest creed.

—Albert Schweitzer

you exist. You will complete a precise and focused statement of your purpose in life, which will stand as a personal testament to what your life is about. It will be your own compelling mission.

Having defined your mission, you will suddenly begin to make connections, to see a pattern to your evolution as a human being. Your life will become less fragmented and more cohesive. What appeared as separate unconnected experiences will gradually merge and blend, creating a fascinating tapestry that is uniquely yours. This mission then becomes your rock, a solid foundation upon which you can create the rest of your life. Who you are and what you do begins to fulfill an even higher purpose: Because of you, the world becomes a better place to live in.

Often counseling about getting what you want from life begins with advice to set goals. Establishing personal goals in all areas of your life is extremely important ,but the next phase of learning to soar builds first upon the principle of contribution: <u>rewards follow service</u>—getting follows giving—and making an impression follows making a difference.

In other words, <u>before determining what it is you want, we need to clarify what It Is you have to offer</u>. In this chapter we are going to define further what is special about you and evolve from that the unique contribution that only you can make to this world.

One note of caution: Patience is essential. The

answers to the questions you must ask yourself rarely come quickly or easily. Because this process requires examining your deepest motives, it often means exploring new territory. This takes time and commitment. Having come this far, however, I know you are ready.

WHY WERE YOU HIRED? In Studs Turkel's best seller, *Working,* he states that work provides both our daily bread and our daily purpose. But does it? For most of us, work consumes so much of our lives that one would hope that it is fulfilling beyond the paycheck.

In a recent survey conducted by the Wilson Learning Corporation, 1,500 people were asked, "If you had enough money to live comfortably for the rest of your life, would you continue to work?" Seventy percent said that they would continue to work, but 60 percent of those said they would change jobs and seek "more satisfying" work.

As an entry point for defining your mission, the first exercise is to clarify the purpose of your current job. The only criteria for answering the following questions are to be honest and to respond as quickly as possible. There are no "right" answers, and over-analyzing can lead to confusion.

Write down three reasons as to:

Why were you hired?

1.

2.

3.

Why did you receive your last promotion? (if applicable)

1.

2.

3.

If you are having trouble answering these questions, try putting yourself in your employer's shoes: Why would you decide to hire a person? What do you think should be the key factors in the decision?

Please complete this exercise before reading further.

It isn't important to come out on top, what matters is to be the one who comes out alive.

–Bertolt Brecht

Every organization, regardless of its level of sophistication, has criteria for making a hiring decision. Once the qualifications and personality of a candidate seem to fit, the final question nearly every employer asks is, Can we see this person contributing in a positive way to the future of our organization?

Therefore, the overriding reason you were hired was that your organization felt that you had a *special contribution* to make to its continuing success. That's the simple yet truthful answer. Why else would you be hired?

Restating that another way, your gifts, talents, expertise, and implied commitment to serve the needs of your employer got you the job.

In *What Color Is Your Parachute?*, a best-selling book for job seekers, Richard Bolles writes, "It doesn't matter what title is hung on a person in order to justify hiring them. They are being hired because in this organization faced with problems, the hiring officer is betting that the new employee will be part of the solution, rather than part of the problem."

In the pressure cooker of daily living, it is easy to lose sight of the primary expectation of employers: contribution. Yet if we care to listen, the message is very clear. Think for a moment of the words that often accompany an award: "For outstanding contribution to the success of. . . ." When we stop contributing, we start our demise.

Richard Bolles poses these significant questions: "<u>The major issue you are facing in the minds of</u> <u>employers is not what skills you have, but to what</u> <u>end and purpose do you set them?</u> Do you use your skills to merely wile away the time? Or do you like to use your skills to solve problems?"

Before moving on, reflect for a few moments on how you have been approaching your work. Go back over your answers to those last questions and try to get in touch with how you would be viewed as a contributor within your organization.

WHY DO YOU WORK? Now let's deal with your *motives* for working. As you respond to the next three questions, remember it is always vitally important to be truthful. As the sage said, "The truth about yourself will set you free."

It is easy to lose sight of the primary expectation of employers: contribution.

Provide at least three answers to each question:

Why do you work?

1.

2.

3.

What does work mean to you?

1.

2.

3.

What do you want from work?

1.

2.

3.

Please complete this exercise before reading further.

I don't want to achieve immortality through my work. I want to achieve it through not dying.

–Woody Allen

Extensive research has been done on the reasons people work. Three reasons seem to overshadow all others.

Money: As a basic motivator, money is certainly effective, especially in our culture. We need to support ourselves and our families. Our ability to do that in no small way determines our self-image. Very few escape the economic pressures of life.

Affiliation: If we look at the world demographically, It becomes obvious that people prefer to cluster in cities or towns. A microcosm of that is the workplace. Feeling connected to others fills a need for belonging, for being with others, as in a team. Work provides the opportunity for helpful feedback, goal setting, recognition, and support.

Meaning: Studies have shown that those who consistently excel at what they do receive far more from work than salary and camaraderie. Today there is growing recognition that productivity is directly linked to the level of satisfaction and fulfillment that people get from their work. People who excel have a sense of purpose, a feeling that their work has meaning and contributes to a worthwhile cause.

Take a moment to look over your answers about why you work. Is there any correlation between your answers and the three factors we've just discussed? How well does your work meet the needs for money, affiliation, and meaning?

Defining your mission is concerned primarily with the *meaning* aspect of your life and work. When your focus is on what you can give rather than get, you will be amazed how the other needs for money and affiliation are met with much less effort.

THE PURPOSE OF YOUR JOB: The purpose of a business (as we have already discussed) is to create and keep customers. There are no organizations, profit or non-profit, that do not have customers in one sense or another. In other words, every organization exists to meet a need and provide a service. Admittedly, the way we are treated by people in some institutions casts some doubt on this last statement, but I believe this results more from a lack of training than anything else.

In this next exercise you will be looking at your job from a marketing perspective. A marketer asks, Who are my customers?

For you, there are two categories of customers: external and internal. External customers are obviously those who purchase products or services or are served in some way by your organization. Internal customers are those within your organization who depend on you for their own job performance. It is very likely that you may never have thought of your fellow workers as customers. Thinking of them as customers, however, can give you not only a fresh perspective on your job, but also bring new meaning and renewed vigor to what you do.

Review the following questions, making notes as answers come to you.

A man is a success if he gets up in the morning and gets to bed at night and in between does what he wants to do.

–Bob Dylan

1. Who are my customers? (Who is affected by my competence and commitment?)

External	Internal

2. What do my customers expect of me? (stated and unstated)

External	Internal

3. What do I offer to meet my customers' expectations? (knowledge, experience, talents, and skills)

External	Internal

There's no labor a man can do that's undignified—if he does it right.

–Bill Cosby

The answers to these questions do not usually come easily. This is because they force you, perhaps for the first time, to think about how you *serve* both the needs of your organization and those you work with. Without this clarity, much of the potential satisfaction that work can offer is lost.

It is understandable if you are experiencing some resistance at this point. Mental exercise is akin to physical exercise. Thinking about doing it and actually doing it are two entirely different things. The latter requires effort. Why make the effort? For no less a reason than life itself, life the way it was meant to be lived—enthusiastically, energetically, and with a positive sense of anticipation.

To help you with this exercise, let's take a look at two examples of answers to the previous questions.

Example 1

Job Title: Vice President—Manufacturing, Building Products Company

1. Who are my customers?

External	Internal
Hardware Store	Salespeople
Builders	Marketing
General Construction Industry	Plant Supervisors

2. What do my customers expect of me? (stated and unstated)

External	Internal
Quality Products	Efficiency
Reliable Service	Flexibility
Friendly & Cooperative	Open & Regular Communication

3. What do I offer to meet my customers' expectations? (knowledge, experience, talents, and skills)

External	Internal
15 Years' Experience in the Industry	Creativity & Ability to Organize
Thorough Understanding of Their Needs	Team Builder & Problem Solver
Innovative & Committed to Quality	Competence & Reliability

Example 2

Job Title: Account Executive, Computer Equipment

1. Who are my customers?

External	Internal
Accountants	Management
Attorneys	Support Staff
Financial Planners	

2. What do my customers expect of me? (stated and unstated)

External	Internal
Indepth Knowledge of Product	Respect for Their Roles
Integrity: Concern for Their Needs	Flexibility
Creativity & Problem Solving	Commitment to the Team

3. What do I offer to meet my customers' expectations? (knowledge, experience, talents, and skills)

External	Internal
10 Years' Success in the Industry	Concern & Appreciation for What They Do
Proven Problem-Solving Capability	Willingness to Listen
Ability to Make Complex Understood	Innovative & Versatile

A school is a place through which you have to pass before entering life, but where the teaching proper does not prepare you for life.

–Ernest Dimnet

Now complete the exercise to the best of your ability before reading further.

The next step is to summarize your answers into one sentence that describes the purpose of your job. What is important in this exercise is not to list your activities and tasks, but rather to identify how your job contributes to your customers and the success of your organization.

Here are concise statements related to the answers given in the two examples:

VICE PRESIDENT: The purpose of my job is to organize and implement the production of the finest quality products in the most cost-effective way, thereby contributing to increased profits, satisfied customers, and the enhanced reputation of the company.

ACCOUNT EXECUTIVE: The purpose of my job is to serve customers by providing innovative solutions to their problems through the use of superior computer technology, thereby contributing to their efficiency and profitability.

The best way to do this exercise is to practice. Write a statement, write another, and another. Then play with the statements, doodle for a while, do whatever is necessary until you have a description that has two elements: It has meaning for you and can provide a clear and concise answer if your boss asked, "What is the purpose of your job?"

Practice Purpose Statements

*Corporations
are social
organizations,
the theater in
which men and
women realize
or fail to realize
purposeful and
productive
lives.*

–Peter Rena

The Purpose of My Job

The distribution of talents in this world should not be our concern. Our responsibility is to take the talents we have and ardently parlay them to the highest possible achievement.

–Alan Loy McGinnis

For the majority of us, work does provide the most significant opportunity to contribute. Gaining a sense of purpose from what we do is therefore a vital first step before tackling what I refer to as the grand task: identifying a life purpose.

WHAT DO YOU DO BEST? Have you ever felt that you were underutilized, that you had far more to offer than was either being asked of you or you were asking of yourself? How about those gifts and talents that have been submerged or that you have been reticent to demonstrate or discuss, perhaps because you wanted to play it safe.

Dick Leider says, "The major problem facing the American worker today is not 'burn-out' but 'rust-out.'" This is the result of a gross underutilization of an individual's potential.

Why does this occur? A primary reason is the fear of risk. In a nation that has produced some of the most brilliant achievers, many of us will suppress or deny our capabilities for the illusion of security. The trade-off for this choice is soul-destroying. Those who have a zest for life are willing to take the risk of pitting their skills and talents against the unknown.

Take a moment to reflect on these questions:

What frame of mind would you like to be in at the beginning of each day?

What feelings would you like to experience at the end of the day?

After you're gone, what would you like people to say about you?

What do you want your life to stand for, to represent?

No matter how you answered them, I am sure that you would not have read this far without my basic assumption about you being true: that, in short, you want to feel *in love* with life.

What this suggests is that you desire the experience of living to be one that you look forward to, have great hopes for, and are in no hurry to see completed. In other words, you have a relationship with life much as you do with the people you are close to and love. They bring you much joy and some sadness, but remain, unquestionably, very precious to you.

Having a love affair with life and avoiding risk are mutually exclusive. The game of life is meant to be played. All active participants win, for the score is unimportant. It is the level of commitment that counts. Observers, the non-risk takers, watch from the sidelines, stimulated only by the fantasy of playing. And then suddenly the game is over.

Defining your mission implies choosing to get in the game. What position shall I play? now becomes the important question. The answer lies in discovering where you are talented and how best to apply those talents.

My life has no purpose, no direction, no aim, no meaning, and yet I'm happy. I can't figure it out. What am I doing right?

—Charles M. Schulz

Consider for a moment a time when you were performing at your best. What were your thoughts and feelings? How did you behave? What were you doing? Write down at least five answers:

1.

2.

3.

4.

5.

It is a funny thing about life; if you refuse to accept anything but the best, you very often get it.

–W. Somerset Maugham

Now consider the opposite, a time when you were doing badly, at your worst. What were your thoughts and feelings? How did you behave? What were you doing? Again, try to come up with five answers:

1.

2.

3.

4.

Life is not a spectacle or feast; it is a predicament.

—George Santayana

5.

Take a look now at what others have said and check out the similarities between your experience and theirs:

At Best	At Worst
Confident	Fearful
Enthusiastic	Apathetic
Organized	Messy
Relaxed	Anxious
Focused	Lacked Direction
In Control	Out of Control
Friendly	Argumentative
Decisive	Frustrated

Although we have all probably experienced the things expressed in both columns, we would prefer to be at our best as much as possible. Therefore, the important question is, What causes us to perform consistently at our best? The answer is profoundly simple: People perform at their best when contributing their talents to something they believe in.

Logic says that any effort to determine our talents and what we believe in will be extremely worthwhile.

The first step is to re-evaluate your special abilities—what you are good at and find easy to do. The following chart is designed for you to list not only your talents but also your assets, skills, and major strengths that you identified in chapter 4.

People perform at their best when contributing their talents to something they believe in.

Take time now to do this, and try to fill up all the spaces provided by freely using your answers from chapter 4 and by adding to them.

My Assets	My Skills

We must see our own goodness, appreciate our assets and abilities, and celebrate our humanness.

–Dennis Wholey

My Talents	My Strengths

No bird soars too high if he soars with his own wings.

–William Blake

Let's pause for a moment to refresh ourselves about what this process is driving at. Our objective is to define a mission for your life that will both function as a source of inspiration and be worthy of your deepest commitment.

This can sound quite serious, even mysterious. But it is really just the clarification of what is important to you. It will provide you with the clear understanding that you do make a difference, that what you do has significance, thereby giving meaning to your existence.

How you contribute: In preparation for this part of the process, it would be wise to find a quiet place where you will not run the risk of being disturbed. The following questions get to the heart of what you want your life to be about. Read these questions carefully and, without writing anything down, reflect on the answers. Just let your mind respond at its own speed. Avoid forcing answers.

How would you like to be remembered?

What have you always dreamed of contributing to the world?

Looking back on your life, what are some of your major contributions?

When people think of you, what might they say are your most outstanding characteristics?

What do you really want from your life and your work?

If answering these questions is requiring you to

stretch, understand that the struggle is normal. *You are choosing to live with purpose and not by accident.* You are taking charge of your life in a way that has profound consequences. Defining your mission transcends any form of goal setting or getting organized. Those are just stepping stones on the path of life. Your mission or purpose is the path itself.

Having reflected, now re-read the questions and put your answers in writing.

Evermore people today have the means to live, but no meaning to live for.

–Victor Frankl

How would you like to be remembered?

What have you always dreamed of contributing to the world?

The work of the individual still remains the spark that moves mankind forward.

–Igor Sikorsky

Looking back on your life, what are some of your major contributions?

When people think of you, what might they say are your most outstanding characteristics?

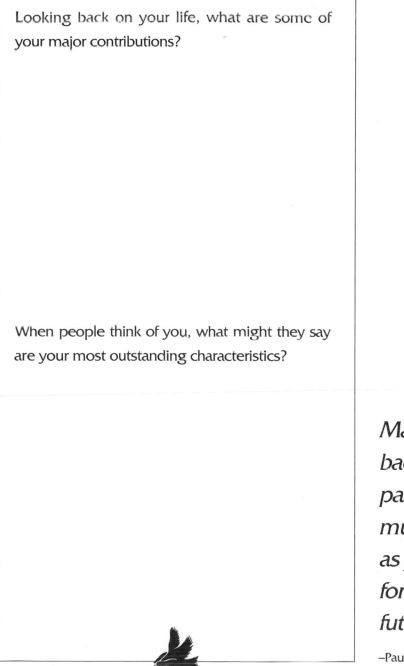

May you look back on the past with as much pleasure as you look forward to the future.

–Paul Dickson

What do you really want from your life and your work?

What the superior man seeks is in himself. What the mean man seeks is in others.

—Confucius

It is time to pull together the discoveries and new awareness you have gathered from the previous exercises. In responding to the next set of questions, feel free to refer back to previous answers, but at the same time, remain open to any new insights.

When a man's willing and eager, the gods join in.

−Aeschylus

What are your strengths? (Check page 97)

What do you most wish to contribute in this next phase of your life? (Check page 100)

What do you want most from your life? (Check page 102)

Remain open to any new insights.

Review for a few moments your answers to these questions. The final exercise is to focus them, to define your mission in a statement of purpose that expresses your commitment to what your life is about.

In preparation, consider some of the characteristics of a purpose.

A Purpose . . .
 . . . focuses on Contribution
 . . . uses Gifts and Talent
 . . . is Meaningful
 . . . is Enjoyable
 . . . is Continuous

Following are some examples of purpose statements. Try to keep your purpose as succinct as possible. But make sure it is also inspiring to you. Your feelings are the best judge of its power and effectiveness.

VICE PRESIDENT–MANUFACTURING: I am helping others to improve the quality of their lives through my special abilities to provide leadership, inspire teamwork, and to direct them in the pursuit of worthy goals.

ACCOUNT EXECUTIVE: I am using my creativeness and a unique ability to communicate to present fresh ideas that have a positive impact on people's lives. Life is to be enjoyed and I help the process.

TEACHER: I am helping children expand their potential and see a bright future through my special talents of listening, encouraging, and bringing out the very best in people.

PHYSICIAN: I am dedicated to improving the quality of health care in the world. I accomplish this through being interested, open, honest, and willing to take a stand for what I believe.

FLIGHT ATTENDANT: I am providing peacefulness to other people. I achieve this by being friendly, helpful, and courteous.

ATHLETE: I am opening up new possibilities for human beings. My special physical and mental gifts are used to promote a spirit of harmony and cooperation among all people.

ATTORNEY: I am helping people manage in a complicated world. My empathy and unique ability to make the difficult understandable provides hope and encouragement to others.

ENTREPRENEUR: I am providing jobs and helping to build a prosperous economy. My ability to motivate people helps them to discover their own potential and opens up an exciting future.

You will observe that the sample statements begin with the words, "I am." This approach is designed to bring an immediate sense of commitment and ownership to your purpose. Used daily as an affirmation, you will discover the fulfillment of

Man is more interesting than men. It's him, not them, whom God made in His image. Each is more precious than all.

—André Gide

your purpose will be automatic.

As you begin this final exercise, remember there are no limits to the number of practice swings permissible. The time clock is not running. Be patient and kind to yourself. This time out lasts as long as is necessary for the description of your purpose to ring true and certain.

Each of our acts makes a statement as to our purpose.

–Leo Buscaglia

Practice Purpose Statements

I am . . .

I am . . .

I am . . .

I am . . .

*Be patient
and kind
to yourself.*

My Purpose Statement

I am . . .

Everybody can be great... because anybody can serve. You don't have to have a college degree to serve. You don't have to make your subject and verb agree to serve... You only need a heart full of grace. A soul generated by love.

—Martin Luther King, Jr.

As you near the end of this chapter, let me demonstrate again some understanding of what you might be experiencing. To those of you who have defined your mission without hesitation: Congratulations!

For the others, perhaps some reassurance is in order. This journey of discovery that you have courageously begun is continuous, and as your awareness grows, your purpose will become clearer and, at times, even change.

There is nothing wrong if your purpose has not revealed itself as clearly as you would like at this point. But I hope you are considerably closer to both knowing what really matters to you and in what direction you want your life to be heading.

It will be worth your while to revisit all the questions asked during this process and check on how you answered them. Sometimes we get caught in the trap of writing how we think we should respond, rather than what we really feel.

The return on any investment of energy and time you put into defining your mission is immeasurable. You will transform, in the most positive sense, how you feel about yourself, your family, and the world.

My purpose is written on a small card that I keep in my wallet. It is my compass, an unfailing guide to the true meaning and possibilities of life.

As is your sort of mind,

So is your sort of search; you'll find

What you desire.

–Robert Browning

Seriously, What Do You Want?

A NEW VISION

Chapter
6

You have now established a worthy purpose—what you want to contribute to the world. The ground is now ready for you to plant the seeds of a new vision, one that will bear only the finest of fruit. It is time to focus on what you want, to turn your dreams into goals so that you are truly able to spend your life in your own way.

The willingness to create a new vision is a statement of your belief in your potential. It is a bold declaration that you are in charge and taking responsibility for your life. It is giving yourself permission to dream once again of what could be and to believe those dreams can come true. With a new vision, you look to the future with positive anticipation rather than nervous apprehension.

Most important, a new vision frees you from the limitations of the past and opens you up to fresh possibilities for your life. It is your taking a stand against the self-doubt and limiting thoughts whose primary intention is to prevent you from breaking through.

Be prepared, however, for as your imagination soars, so might doubt try to shoot you down with a cynical, How are you going to do that? Ignore the doubt and put aside the *how* at this point. If you can decide what it is you really want and summon the belief that *somehow* it is possible, then you can accomplish it.

Terry Fox met many cynics and doubters when he

There is only one success— To be able to spend your life in your own way.

—Christopher Morley

chose as his goal to run across Canada and to raise a million dollars for cancer research. "What have you done on two legs, let alone the one you now have?" they implied. In the beginning, he, too, was unsure of the *how,* but he finally answered them—not in words but action, by running the greatest marathon in history and raising over $24 million.

What many people fail to grasp is how the *principle of contribution* works. Their lives are so consumed with getting rather than giving that they just survive in a world of abundance. They get little because they give little. Again, quoting from *Soundings:*

"Why is it," said a rich man to his minister, "that people call me stingy when everyone knows that when I die I'm leaving everything to this church?"

"Let me tell you the story of the pig and the cow," said the minister. "The pig was unpopular and the cow was beloved. This puzzled the pig. 'People speak warmly of your gentle nature and your soulful eyes,' the pig said to the cow. 'They think you're generous because each day you give them milk and cream. But what about me? I give them everything I have. I give bacon and ham. I provide bristles for brushes. They even pickle my feet! Yet no one likes me. Why is that?'

"Do you know what the cow answered?" said the minister. "She said, 'Perhaps it's because I give while I'm still living.'"

I hope you will now allow this principle to work

for you, for you have gained the knowledge that *rewards follow service,* and so you are free to serve well. By remaining faithful to the principle, you will be astonished by what eventually comes your way, for it is impartial—it plays no favorites. It does not value one contribution over another or prefer one reward over another. Eventually you will discover, like so many others, its generosity, for you will receive far in excess of what you have given.

Even so, it is wise to acknowledge that to create a new vision takes courage. The fear of failure is for many people an insurmountable obstacle to stepping out into an unknown future no matter how exciting and gratifying its promise.

The encouragement I give you is that people who realize their dreams are not without fears but are people willing to move forward in the face of fear. Obstacles lie in their path as with anyone else, but they understand that surmounting these obstacles is a part of the game and, ironically, part of the reward.

What you are must always displease you, if you would attain to that which you were not.

–St. Augustine

That you are willing to advance in the direction of your dreams is testimony to your courage. Immediately you are distinguishable from those whose fears have caused their minds to stagnate into a form of mental atrophy. Their desires are numb and existence bland, for they have shut down their imaginations by buying the *lie of limitation.*

Let us begin the process of creating a new vision.

With total honesty, answer the following:

In what way may you still feel limited by the past? If so, by what?

What will it take to let go of what has happened, no matter how good or bad? Are you willing to let go?

Today's opportunities erase yesterday's failures.

–Gene Brown

How might the rut of conformity or comfort be limiting you? Why?

How different do you really want life to be? Why?

Nothing will ever be attempted, if all possible objections must first be overcome.

–Samuel Johnson

Have you ever stated what it is you truly desire?
If not, why not?

How good could you stand life to be? Explain?

You have to move up to another level of thinking, which is true for me and everybody else. Everybody has to learn to think differently, bigger, to be open to possibilities.

–Oprah Winfrey

It often happens that I wake up at night and begin to think about a serious problem and decide I must tell the Pope about it. Then I wake up completely and remember that I am the Pope.

—Pope John XXIII

Having reflected on your answers, consider now some common barriers that keep people from getting what they want. One, or more of these, may have surfaced as you answered the previous questions.

The first barrier is the lack of awareness that we have considerable influence over the outcomes of our lives. Despite the enormous amount of information available on the subject, it is often a major revelation that successful people are not just lucky but have planned, designed, and worked extremely hard for their place in the world. As hinted at earlier, even if the truth is evident, a deliberate ignorance makes it much easier for some to continue to play victim and envy the good fortune of others rather than summon up what is necessary to take charge of their lives and create their own good fortune.

A second barrier is the feeling of being undeserving of fulfilling our dreams. It is the result of misinformed decisions about ourselves, based on erroneous data, that communicate a sense of unworthiness whenever we dare to look at good things for our lives. Any message of this nature, as we have already discussed, is entirely false. Understand and accept that your heritage as a member of the human family is the right to participate in this game of life at any level and in any form you desire.

A third barrier is cultural. It has to do with how we define or measure success. I do believe you can accomplish what your heart desires, but I take issue with those who suggest those desires always have to be big in a material sense to be worth anything. If they are truly what you want, if they motivate you to action, if they have enough pull to get you up when you feel like sleeping in, if they stretch your known capacities, and if they are worthy of you in that they represent what your heart and soul are saying, then they are great goals no matter how big or small they appear. Guidance from others can be helpful, but only you can decide the priorities in your life.

This is not intended to limit your dreams and goals in any way. If you can clearly visualize what it is you want and believe that you have the capability of achieving it, and if you are willing to invest both the necessary time and mental and physical energy in getting it, then you can have it.

What we value and desire most, however, varies from person to person and often changes throughout the various stages of life. The same intensity of desire can exist within two people with very different goals. One is motivated by seeing himself as the CEO of an international company while the other gets excited about taking a sabbatical to write a novel, often for no other reason than personal satisfaction. *Always, always, always, be true to yourself.*

Always, always, always be true to yourself.

From my own story so far, you can appreciate that for much of my early life the goals I set were substantially in the big category, at least in terms of how the world would define them. In other words, they related to acquiring and having things, for my thinking at that time led me to believe that the acquisitions led to being "somebody."

After my first business failed and when I finally altered course from the road to oblivion, I set a goal that perhaps is a good example of big being relative. It was a most critical and important goal and took four years to achieve. I shall never forget the day of victory.

At a meeting with my accountants, they produced a statement that had on it the good news. It was a balance sheet of my assets and liabilities and the bottom line indicated that my net worth was now absolutely nothing. To understand the significance of this accomplishment is to appreciate the debt accumulated by my business had been substantial and that every cent owed to my creditors was paid back. Having a zero net worth is not generally considered cause for celebration in our society, but it was a most worthy and, in retrospect, very humorous achievement for me.

But the biggest goal I ever set in my life, in terms of importance and for whose accomplishment I shall be forever grateful and thankful, was the reconcilia-

Not only must you know what you want, but you must really want what you want, if you are to get what you want.

tion with my family. There was no treasure on earth more valuable to me than this.

Not only must you know what you want, but you must really want what you want, if you are to get what you want. Getting my family back became my magnificent obsession as I dared to dream what, to many who knew us, felt was an impossible dream. In the beginning, the how it was to be achieved was completely unknown, but I believed it was possible and could clearly see us all together again.

To grasp the importance of this believing without an apparent *how* is to understand that the mind attracts the physical representation of that which it holds as an image. It works by subconsciously guiding you into the correct actions to bring about the manifestation of your vision.

To achieve my goal, I made painful and painstaking inquiries into the causes of the problems between my wife and me. Having discovered answers, I then made definite changes in my attitudes and behavior. Fortunately, my wife, in accepting responsibility for her own part in the breakdown, was following the same process.

Time, then, had to do its work. As the blaming ceased and the anger dissipated, forgiveness healed the hurts. Love was then able to surface and be nurtured again. It was finally the very real and positive changes we had both committed to and experienced

All marriages are happy. It's the living together afterward that causes all the trouble.

–Raymond Hull

in each other, however, that gave us the courage to begin what would become an entirely new relationship.

Extracts from my life are shared with you for two reasons. The first is that the recovery from financial distress and marital reconciliation revealed to me the actual purpose of goal setting. The primary reward is not the goal but what you become as a result of doing all that was necessary to reach the goal. You become a more powerful and effective human being.

The second reason is that, as you create your new vision, it will be multi-faceted. Wisdom is understanding the need for balance in our lives, and so your goals will include not only those that involve career, but also family, friends, health, and the spiritual dimension of your life.

Again, this is not meant to suggest in any way that you should limit your vocational and career aspirations, for in every field of endeavor we need those who are willing to break through into new realms of possibility. The mere fact that you are a human being, however, means that attention to family, friends, and soul is essential to experiencing fully the potential joy and fulfillment in life.

Creating a new vision starts with laying out everything you have dared to imagine for your life. *So let us begin.* In the next ten minutes give permission to your imagination to run wild and free. As all those desires, dreams, hopes, and fantasies come into your mind, write them down. Remember, no one else is watching, and these are not commitments, but possibilities.

Everything starts as somebody's daydream.

–Larry Niven

The soul...
never thinks
without a
picture.

–Aristotle

Congratulations! You have managed the vital first step that so many are unwilling to take. At this stage, it might be difficult to comprehend, but the how of fulfilling your dreams is nowhere near as challenging as being willing to admit to and clarify them in the first place.

All dreams need not be the stuff of which history is made. Most are very personal. Parents dream of the kind of person their child might be someday. Entrepreneurs dream of success in the marketplace, of a better product, a better way to deliver a service. To be alive is to dream. And yet, in the daily pursuit of our dreams we cannot avoid challenges— and our approach to struggle invariably mirrors our approach to the most significant.

–Stephan M. Wolf

Now it is time to separate what you have written on the previous two pages into four categories. They are: Personal, Career, Family, and Spiritual. The latter is defined as anything you have wanted to do that focuses on nourishing your spirit.

Personal:

Career:

*What a man
can be,
he must be.
This need
we call self-
actualization.*

–Abraham Maslow

Family:

Spiritual:

Other things may change us, but we start and end with family.

–Anthony Brandt

After you have separated your list, take each category and prioritize what you have written into ten-, five-, and one-year goals. At this time be honest and eliminate any you could identify as fantasies that have no dynamic pull or appeal. No matter how grand, keep all the items in each category you would love to achieve. Be realistic, however, as to the time frame so as to keep them believable. Goals should stretch you but not to the breaking point.

Now prioritize these in terms of how strongly they attract. *A* would represent most desirable, *B* very desired, *C* desired, and so on all the way to *Z* if you have that many.

Next, take the *As* from each of your one-, five-, and ten-year goals and write them in the spaces provided.

Think like a man of action, act like a man of thought.

–Henri Bergson

One Year:

Five Year:

Ten Year:

The method of the enterprising is to plan with audacity and execute with vigor.

–Christian Bovee

While we are here we should set goals and achieve them, make the best of things, make others feel good about themselves, and be happy with what we are and what we are doing.

–Janet Evans

It is important now to put these three *A* goals to the test. Why do you want them? Answer the following questions:

I want my one-year *A* goal because:

I want my five-year *A* goal because:

I want my ten-year *A* goal because:

Take a few minutes to reflect on your answers and assess the intensity of your desire for these goals. If you have doubts about your willingness to commit to achieving anyone of them, then review other goals in that category and select another for this "test." Process your list until you have those you feel strongest about.

Take some more time now to assess your overall feelings toward these exercises. No feeling is invalid. The adrenalin of excitement could be pumping, fear could be present, or perhaps a quiet sense of satisfaction from finally clarifying what it is you want from life. Accept these feelings and consider that whatever goal you have written down, it is yours. The time frame you have set for its attainment is only an estimate. You will be wonderfully surprised by how some goals will be attained much sooner than expected, but you must be flexible enough not to give up on those that, for unforeseen circumstances, take longer.

Treat your goals as guides. They should stretch and challenge you but not defeat you. They are moving targets that require patience and persistence if we are to hit them with consistency. There is no guarantee of reaching a goal at a certain time, but there is a guarantee of never attaining goals that are never set.

Through your willingness to admit to your

Treat your goals as guides. They should stretch and challenge you but not defeat you.

dreams and establish a clear vision for your life, you have now applied for membership in the exclusive club of the achiever. Final acceptance will be determined ultimately by your actions.

Terry Fox's noble purpose of raising money for cancer research, together with the breathtaking goal of running across Canada, would have been meaningless without his willingness to spend fourteen months in preparation and training followed by the daily, relentless pursuit of his dream. Terry knew that the world is full of people with good intentions, but what makes dreams come true are positive, goal-oriented actions.

Terry's run was described as "a triumph of the human spirit." His message, however, was that this same spirit exists in all of us. All that is required to bring it forth, he stated, is a "good goal to fight for."

What makes dreams come true are positive, goal-oriented actions.

You now have those good goals to fight for, so take action and write down something you could do toward each of your goals during the next twenty-four hours that would demonstrate and leave no doubt that you really want to achieve them

One Year:

Five Year:

Ten Year:

What a man is is the basis of what he dreams and thinks, accepts and rejects, feels and perceives.

–John Mason Brown

Finally, identify an action step for each goal, no matter how small, that could move you forward immediately! Like right now, say, "Hey, I'm on my way!"

One Year:

Five Year:

It is better to create than to be learned; creating is the true essence of life.

–Reinhold Neibuhr

Ten Year:

With the inspiration of a worthy purpose and now the motivation of exciting goals, you do not have to settle for anything less than what you want.

It is my experience that, as with the statement of purpose for my life, my new vision needs to be reviewed and affirmed daily. It has also been transferred to a card that I keep in my wallet. As I reflect on my goals, I can then effectively prioritize my day to remove the distractions that would alter my course.

Enthusiasm for life is the spirit within that Terry Fox experienced. It is activated by being involved with and working toward that which is meaningful to us. Clarity of intention or focus, propelled by enthusiasm, is the most potent combination known to humankind. It is the genesis of all accomplishment; it is the key characteristic that bonds all those who take charge of their lives and set the course of their own futures.

Welcome to the club!

Appollanaire said

"Come to the edge."

"It's too high."

"Come to the edge."

"We might fall."

"Come to the edge."

And they came.

And he pushed them.

And they flew.

–Christopher Hogue

TAKING CHARGE
OF YOUR THOUGHTS

ATTITUDE

CHAPTER
7

You have now placed yourself in a special and rare category of people. It is the uncommon person who knows not only what he or she wants from life, but also what he or she has to offer and contribute to it.

With your new vision you have generated a clear, positive expectation about life and have much to look forward to, to be excited about. That is a fundamental key to happiness. Establishing an inspiring purpose, one that leaves no doubt about why you are here, is another.

Now we must examine what it will actually take to live the life you imagine for yourself.

Despite all the good work we have done so far, it would be folly to believe that we can control everything that happens in our lives. Much of the pain and frustration we experience is the result of resistance to that which is not only out of our control, but also what we feel is unfair or should not happen to us. If we can replace this resistance with acceptance, stop judging and start learning from the unpredictable events of our lives, we begin to discover another key to happiness.

Goals, if they are to be reached, certainly require careful planning and follow through, but it would be arrogant and misguided to think that there should or would not be any strong challenges to those plans along the way. To not have the flexibility to alter our plans and reset our goals is potentially to set our-

Vote with your life. Vote Yes!

–Das Energi

selves up for failure. Our vision becomes a prison.

There are times also when, to accomplish a particular task or goal, unwavering concentration not only is necessary but also imperative. Many of life's true joys, however, often present themselves at unexpected, supposedly inconvenient times. If our daily existence is so rigidly organized and planned that an interesting, spontaneous detour is not permissible, we will find ourselves living a life of joyless achievement.

A recent cover story in *Time* magazine was entitled, "How America Has Run Out of Time." The emphasis was on how technology, rather than fulfilling its promise to free us up, seems somehow to have made time an even more precious commodity as we rush to do more. The story concluded: "At some point individuals must find the time to consider the price of their preoccupation and the toll on the spirit exacted by exhaustion. With too little sleep there are too few dreams. . . . Some things are just worth the time."

Most of this book was written in the early hours of the morning. This creative time was very important and precious to me. Occasionally one of my children, sleepy eyed and drowsy, would come looking for her dad wondering why he was awake when "it's still dark out there." My inclination was to send her back to bed, but then I would have missed out on this little person snuggling into and cuddling me. How long will she be little? I put down my pen and gave thanks for being so loved.

I believe this anonymous poem demonstrates an enlightened attitude toward the scheduling of our daily lives:

Take time to work—
> *It is the price of success.*
Take time to think—
> *It is the source of power.*
Take time to play—
> *It is the secret of perpetual youth.*
Take time to read—
> *It is the fountain of wisdom.*
Take time to be friendly—
> *It is the road to happiness.*
Take time to love and be loved—
> *It is nourishment for the soul.*
Take time to share—
> *It is too short a life to be selfish.*
Take time to laugh—
> *It is the music of the heart.*
Take time to dream—
> *It is hitching your wagon to a star.*

No matter how wonderful the future may look to you at this time, you must now place your feet firmly on the ground of the present moment. You create a productive, loving life by creating productive, loving

Half our life is spent trying to find something to do with the time we have rushed through life trying to save.

–Will Rogers

moments. The experience of productive, loving moments is determined more by your attitude than anything else.

Your attitude is the way you think about your life and all it contains. It is your approach to and perspective on life. It influences your actions and reactions. It affects your relationships with others and your relationship to yourself. Because your attitude reflects your thinking, It Is the beginning point of creation. Possibilities and limitations are, first and foremost, residents of the mind, and both are released by your attitude.

Those who learn to soar have the courage to take a *positive* attitude toward life. They understand that life offers many surprises but believe that within those surprises are lessons—and that from the lessons comes wisdom. A positive attitude requires courage because it is a decision not to be defeated no matter what challenges life presents.

A positive attitude is like the oil in an engine. It is the lubricant that enables the mind's creative, solution-oriented power to respond to your command. A negative attitude drains the mind of this essential lubricant, freezing and shutting it down. A positive attitude sees a problem as an opportunity, a difficulty as a challenge. A negative attitude does the opposite and is the prescription for defeat.

A positive attitude is a common target for the

cynical whose perspective of life is the result of unful-filled expectations leading to disillusionment. Theirs is a reality that would view Christopher Nolan's lot in life as unjust. Fortunately, Christopher chose to see it differently and, because of his positive approach to life, his incredible talent is changing the world.

For Christopher Nolan, writing is almost a super-human task, often taking him a quarter of an hour to write just one word. Born with severe cerebral palsy that left his body practically useless, he spends much of his life strapped into a wheelchair, for his face and limbs are subject to uncontrollable spasms. He is devoid of speech and, until the age of eleven, when he learned to type, Christopher was locked in a mute world of his own. Only family and close friends could understand his one method of communication: subtle shifts of brightly blinking eyes.

Without further investigation, the immediate reaction to such a story is pity, but Christopher Nolan would denounce that sentiment as false and destruc-tive. From his viewpoint, such sympathy emanates from the narrow perspective of the "able bodied" person who, in the main, assumes that anything less than physical normality is wrong, perhaps even a tragedy.

His is a story of triumph, however, for as I write these words Christopher Nolan, at twenty-two years of age, is already being hailed as a literary genius.

Supported by unrelenting parental love, incredible personal desire, and the wonders of modern technology, he has transcended the severe physical limitations of his life and has brought to the world an irreverent, moving, and breathtakingly honest style of writing that is inspiring all those privileged to know of him.

Recently honored with Britain's coveted Whitbread Prize for his autobiography *Under the Eye of the Clock,* his work is being compared to writers such as James Joyce and W. B. Yeats.

The words of Christopher's mother, Bernadette, tell us what we need to hear: "He has shown them that life is worth living, and it doesn't matter whether you're in a wheelchair or a bed; it's what's going on in your mind and soul that is important."

There is more to learn from this remarkable young man. In his autobiography, written in the third person, Christopher takes us back to when he was three and tells of the day when he cried bitterly upon realizing he was not like other children. But it was . . . "once, once only . . ." for ". . . looking through his tears he saw his mother . . ." who ". . . for the rest of his life would . . . challenge him to think positively."

"Listen here," she said, "you can see, you can hear, you can understand everything you hear, you like your food, you like nice clothes, you are loved by me and Dad. We love you just as you are."

Pain nourishes courage. You can't be brave if you've only had wonderful things happen to you.

–Mary Tyler Moore

Christopher goes on to share his response to his mother's loving but honest words: "The decision arrived at that day was burnt forever in his mind. He was only three years in age, but he was now fanning the only spark he saw, his being alive and more immediate, his being wanted just as he was. . . . That day looked out through his eyes for the rest of his life. His clumsy body was his. . . . He looked . . . at his limbs and liked [himself]."

He liked himself. How important a decision that was! It did not mean a miraculous cure of his disability, but the effect was perhaps even more stunning. It was at that very moment he began to shift his attention away from his limitations and focus on what was possible, what he could do with his life. He began to listen to the phenomena exploding inside his head. He explains it this way: "My mind is just like a spin dryer at full speed. My thoughts fly around my skull, while millions of beautiful words cascade down into my lap. Images gunfire across my consciousness and, while trying to discipline them, I jump in awe at the soul-filled beauty of mind's expanse."

I first discovered Christopher Nolan when reading an interview with him published in *The Christian Science Monitor.* To them goes my deep gratitude and acknowledgement for much of what I have quoted. However, now comes a response by Christopher that literally shocked me out of some ingrained assump-

If you keep on saying things are going to be bad, you have a good chance of being a prophet.

–Isaac Bashevis Singer

tions and views on life.

His mother explains his incredible attitude: "He's telling you that . . . we instinctively judge his life by looking at it through our able-bodied eyes and we almost see it as a failure, a tragedy. But to him, it isn't like that at all; it's just life! It's as normal to him, as grand to him, as complete for him, as our able-bodied lives are to us."

How powerful! If we can fully grasp the significance, the implications of these words, then we can come to terms with our own unique place in the universe. We can shift our focus from distorted images of what is perfect, fun, and beautiful. We can begin to understand that what is truly magnificent is the person who, no matter what cards of life he or she was dealt, still wins because the game is played with acceptance, intelligence, wit, humor, and integrity.

Finally, we can let go of our own if onlys, perceived missing pieces, dissatisfactions, comparisons, and judgments, and like Christopher Nolan, our spirit will then be triumphant over that which would disable us from plowing through life at the full throttle of our capabilities.

She had been through treatment once but apparently had not got the message for she was still drinking. The mother of four, divorced from a successful lawyer and now struggling to maintain a home and, most important, her dignity, she was unfortunately losing the battle; the booze was her escape. Then one evening after a tiring day at work, Mary came home to an empty house. On the kitchen table was a bottle of scotch with a note attached to it. It was a "gift" from her children, but the note read, "If this is the way you want to kill yourself, go ahead, but you're not killing us!" The kids had abandoned her.

This time the treatment worked, but for twelve months she struggled with the stream of insights and revelations about her life and why she had become an alcoholic. The thought did occur to her that she might be crazy, but she certainly was not.

Mary has built her life one day at a time by choosing every morning to look positively at the world no matter what would come her way. It has not been easy. She got her children back only to lose one of them in a drowning accident.

Today, however, she is an inspiration to the many people who have benefited from the organization she founded, The Center for Creative Family Living. Both adults and children are being shown how to take charge of and be responsible for their lives. In Mary's words, "There is a better way."

When we are unable to find tranquility within ourselves, it is useless to seek it elsewhere.

–La Rochefoucauld

A positive attitude does not dissolve life's problems; rather, it is an effective, constructive approach to dealing with them. The positive thinker accepts life as it unfolds without trying to control it or have it conform to limited human expectations. The positive thinker regards life as an adventure where the rewards are in the risks and the pleasure in responding to the challenge.

Whether life is a privilege or a pain has nothing to do with the circumstances of our lives; it is a direct reflection of our attitudes. As difficult, as painful, and as unpredictable as life can be, it cannot defeat us unless we choose to be defeated.

Those who have a positive attitude have a far deeper understanding of how life works than those who do not. It is the negative thinker who cannot grasp that the journey through life has many twists and turns that cannot be foreseen but through which we all have to travel. It is the negative thinker who fights the journey with excuses and rationalizations while failing to realize that it is his frantic resistance that is causing more turbulence.

A positive attitude is a choice. Life gives us a certain physical appearance, and we choose to accept it and make the most of it. The day throws out a problem, and we mentally reposition it into a challenge to wrestle with and to solve. It has been said that the more problems you have the more alive you are.

Getting out of bed on the right side every morning requires not only physical but mental effort as well. Exercising, eating a healthy breakfast, starting the day with an expression of love to someone special are signs about what is going on in our minds. Plato said, "Take charge of your thoughts. You can do what you will with them."

This is not Pollyannish. This is not being out of touch with reality. This is courageous. It is also the only way you can afford to think if you are to manifest the vision you have for your life.

In the chapter on self-appreciation, we discussed the importance of letting go of the past and getting to a full appreciation of every facet of who you are. The purpose of that work was to provoke, challenge, and focus your thinking so that you can understand and accept that you have all the equipment you need for your unique journey through life. Whether that equipment is ever used, however, will depend on your attitude.

No one has ever lived your life before, no one has or will face your challenges, and no one can take your place. You have the courage. The spirit exists within you, and it will triumph through your taking a positive attitude.

A happy person is not a person in a certain set of circumstances, but rather a person with a certain set of attitudes.

–Hugh Downs

MAY THE FORCE BE WITH YOU

COMMITMENT

CHAPTER
8

Benjamin Disraeli became the Prime Minister of Great Britain in the early part of this century. Disraeli's goal was thought impossible to achieve for he was a Jew and anti-Semitism was rampant in that country. Those who opposed him were rich, powerful, and aggressive, and their tactics were less than honorable. How then did he succeed?

Terry Fox had planned his run meticulously. His training had indicated that a daily objective of twenty-six miles was within his capabilities. Unforeseen, however, were the unseasonable weather conditions that seemed to conspire to hold him back: severe headwinds, heavy rain, snow, and icy roads. One month out he had managed to struggle to an average of only eight miles per day. Why did he keep going?

> *Nothing can withstand the power of the human will if it is willing to stake its very existence to the extent of its purpose.*
>
> –Benjamin Disraeli

The answer to both of these questions is *commitment.* Commitment is the willingness to do whatever it takes to get what you want. A true commitment is a heartfelt promise to yourself from which you will not back down. Many people have dreams and many have good intentions but few are willing to make the commitment necessary for their attainment.

You now face a significant moment of truth. No matter how noble your purpose, how clear your vision, or how positive your attitude, what you have envisioned for your future will remain a dream, a fantasy, unless you are willing to take a stand, to be committed.

Now would be a good time to review the statement of purpose for your life. Ask yourself, How badly do I want to fulfill that purpose? What does it really mean to me? Do I really believe I can make that much of a difference?

Now review your new vision. Ask yourself, How strongly do I desire those goals? What will achieving them mean to me? Are they believable? What price am I willing to pay to make them come true?

As I write these words, the Olympic Games are taking place. Like Disraeli and Fox, the athletes are, perhaps, extreme examples of commitment. Even so, they model what is necessary to succeed. Your aspirations may not be as far reaching as theirs; nonetheless, the ability to achieve your goals will be determined proportionately by the level to which you are willing to be committed.

Commitment influences behavior, and behavior determines results. If we are committed to our health, we will exercise and consume that which nourishes the body. If we are committed to our family, we will spend time with them. If we are committed to our vocation and career, we will continually seek ways to improve the quality of our work.

There's a difference between interest and commitment. When you're interested in doing something, you do it only when it's convenient. When you're committed to something, you accept no excuses, only results.

–Kenneth Blanchard

The need for commitment comes from the presence of two phenomena that accompany those who march forward with a great purpose and vision for their lives. The first is *resistance.* It seems that any accomplishment of substance that is worthwhile and lasting is only available at the end of some sort of struggle.

Resistance can take many forms: family, friends, advisers, self-doubt, self-defeating habits, lack of money, regulations, narrow thinking, dishonesty, isolation, and lack of support—plus numerous other unforeseen difficulties. These can leave you puzzled and questioning whether you should continue in your quest or if you are out of touch with reality.

Take comfort in that this is an experience shared by all those who seek to shape their destinies and move beyond mediocrity. There appears to be a direct correlation between the power of an idea and the amount of resistance to it. Albert Einstein stated: "Great spirits have always encountered violent opposition from mediocre minds." Commitment is the enemy of resistance for it is the serious promise to press on, to get up, no matter how many times you are knocked down.

Commitment is also the parent of determination, and determination is one quality you will find common in the lives of all successful people. Commitment as manifested in determined action is the fuel

A true commitment is a heartfelt promise to yourself from which you will not back down.

that will propel you into the future you have imagined for yourself.

The Los *Angeles Times* published a report recently on a five-year study of 120 of America's top artists, athletes, and scholars. Benjamin Bloom, a University of Chicago education professor who led the team of researchers, said, "We expected to find tales of great natural gifts. We didn't find that at all. Their mothers often said it was their other child who had the greater gift." The study concluded that the <u>key element common to all of these successful people was, surprisingly, not talent but an extraordinary drive and determination.</u>

Only you can decide whether the rewards you look forward to are worth the effort, for the truth is, there are tradeoffs. You can't have a healthy body and live on junk food. The security of a guaranteed salary is non-existent when you start your own business. Television and straight As are rare companions.

Successful people refer to commitment as "paying your dues." What does this mean? We leave the concert or ballet thrilled with the performance and marvelling at the artistry. Do we ever consider, however, the endless hours of practice and rehearsal, the buckets of perspiration that made possible such a joyous experience?

The movie is over and we have laughed or cried, jumped out of our skin or cringed, wondered at the

Always bear in mind that your own resolution to succeed is more important than any one thing.

—Abraham Lincoln

special effects or the many other aspects of the art of film making. Do we appreciate the number of rehearsals of each scene in order to get everything just right, followed then by months of long hours in the editing room putting together a final product that provides such wonderful entertainment?

The glory of the Olympics fills our living rooms, and we watch in awe celebrating the triumph of the athletes. Do we ever think about the thousands of hours spent on the track with few observers, often in inclement weather, the injuries, defeats, and the lack of a normal social life, indeed the many sacrifices that must be made to participate in the world's greatest sporting event?

No one can arrive from being talented alone. God gives talent; work transforms talent into genius.

–Anna Pavlova

An adventurer is the only apt description for Mike Plant. He had traveled much of the world by his mid-twenties with excursions into remote places that only the courageous or foolhardy would attempt to enter.

An avid sailor since he was a boy, Mike was now in Jamestown, Rhode Island, doing construction work and enjoying the sea whenever possible. Having reached his thirties, life seemed to be passing him by, and he was hungry for a challenge, an opportunity to stretch himself.

One night a local theater showed a documentary about the BOC Challenge, an around the world solo yacht race. Mike was there and he was hooked. There was no question that he wanted to be a participant in the next race that was then two years away. For Mike, this would truly test his capabilities.

Friends and family were still working on the boat when the starting gun went off. Nothing had been easy. Only minimal sponsorship had been available, and so the boat had literally been built by Mike and anybody else he could get to volunteer or to work on the faith that money would eventually come in.

He set out ill-equipped technologically, in comparison to the other boats, but it did not matter, for he was in the race and that was his dream. The voyage took eight months, and during that time a dear friend and competitor was lost at sea. That was the only time he got close to giving up.

Mike won his division of the race, and he is very proud. If you ever meet him, however, you will notice he has no airs and regards himself as just an ordinary human being. He is a talented, knowledgeable, and skillful sailor but it is his "never give up" attitude that made his extraordinary achievement possible.

My intention throughout our work together has always been to be honest with you. That is why I endeavor to balance the new possibilities for your life with the truth about what it will take to reach them. Commitment is the mental resolve never to give up. Determined action is the evidence of that resolve. Success requires both mental and physical effort.

If this sounds like hard work, consider the alternative, the life of the uncommitted. For them, there is no compelling reason to get up in the morning or to rest at night. One day follows another with the only goal being survival. The uncommitted vacillate on the smallest of decisions and make mountains out of molehills to alleviate their boredom. They have tragically given up on what they were capable of becoming. They pay a far greater price: They have sold out their heritage.

Many times I have been asked, "How can you be so sure that if people commit themselves they will get what they want?" There are two aspects to my response.

The first takes us back to what I believe is the purpose of life: to grow and contribute. Neither should stop until we take our last breath. If growth and contribution is our primary mission in life, then our commitment must be to follow the paths that lead us to the fulfillment of that mission. Some of these paths, however, may turn out to be different from what we originally envisioned. As we cannot predict the future, choosing a direction should therefore always include a positive option: Either this or something better. Openness and flexibility ensures you always get what is best for you.

The second aspect of the answer deals with the second of the phenomena that accompanies the committed person: *synchronicity.* Synchronicity is a meaningful coincidence. The purpose of synchronicity is to encourage, for the coincidence occurs most often when resistance has weakened our resolve. Put another way, synchronicity is the attraction of circumstances into our lives that clearly support the accomplishment of that which we desire.

Terry Fox has played a very important part in my life. *The Power of Purpose* is a film that I had the privilege to produce and that I hope is a fitting legacy to what Terry's life was about. As I endeavored to make this film, I experienced both phenomena of resistance and synchronicity.

Although I had never been involved with film making before, I had some knowledge about what was technically required. I estimated that the project from start to finish should take six months. The commitment I felt was total, for Terry's was a story that deserved to be recorded for history. It was certainly to me a compelling mission.

A major surprise was in store for me, however, in the guise of multiple unforeseen obstacles and unexpected resistance. Although I knew my intentions were honorable, those whose cooperation I needed to complete the project were highly suspicious and distrusting. This was not the result of anything I had personally done, but so many people had tried, often insensitively, to exploit Terry's name for personal gain.

The three things I admired most about Terry were his integrity, his purpose, and his commitment. I was to be thoroughly tested in each of those arenas before the film was finally made.

The project took three years.

You can't always get what you want,

you can't always get what you want.

But, if you try real hard,

you just might get what you need.

—The Rolling Stones

A dilemma I faced was that I had no desire to offend or to go against the wishes of Terry's family, yet no one else was making an effort to produce an educational film about Terry, such as the one I had conceived. Home Box Office produced *The Terry Fox Story,* but that was a re-enactment that lacked some factual accuracy. The Canadian Broadcasting Commission released a documentary that was a chronicle of Terry's run, but its purpose was to relate events not his message.

Any discouragement I felt after the many rejections was countered by the support and encouragement of those who knew what I was endeavoring to do and who did not want me to give up.

There were a few times, however, when the resistance level was so high that I was ready to call an end to the project. At each of these times an incredible *meaningful coincidence* occurred, leaving me with no doubt that I should press on.

One such coincidence left me in complete awe of the phenomenon of synchronicity.

If at first you do succeed—try to hide your astonishment.

—Harry F. Banks

The project was at the two-and-a-half-year mark. It seemed that at last I had broken through, and the film would go ahead. Terry's parents had finally written, through their lawyer, to say they had no objection to the project, and the Canadian Cancer Society had previously suggested that, if Terry's family were in agreement, it would also cooperate by giving me access to the film footage they had of Terry.

I flew to Toronto to meet with the Cancer Society and their attorneys for what I thought would be the signing of a contract. The meeting began with their putting several new obstacles in my way. Stunned and hurt, I found myself with little to say. I left quite quickly after stating that I would get back to them, but I decided to give up. I had had enough.

"It was not worth it," I told myself, "If they cannot understand what I'm trying to do after all this time, the film is obviously not meant to be made." I headed for the airport to catch the first flight home feeling angry, confused, and not wanting anyone to intrude on my anger.

The journey back to Minneapolis involved changing planes in Detroit. I completed the first leg of the journey victorious; I had not uttered one word to anybody. The second plane was fairly empty, but a young woman, whom I later discovered was seventeen years old, was sitting in the same row.

As a strong hint that I did not wish to communicate, I immediately picked up the airline magazine, held it just a few inches from my face, and stared at it intensely. My behavior made no impression, for shortly after take off she asked, "Going to Minneapolis?"

"This is a non-stop flight to Minneapolis; where the heck else could I be going?" I thought. Without moving my head a fraction I answered, "Yes!"

A few moments later she asked, "Do you live in Minneapolis?"

My second answer: "Yes."

After many more questions it became obvious that this young woman was more determined to have a conversation than I was to ignore her. Her persistence and warmth seeped through my cold exterior. Finally, I felt obligated to ask her a few questions.

Me: "Do you like flying?"

Her: "Yes." Pause. "But it's a little awkward for me."

Me: "What do you mean it's a little awkward?"

Her: "Well, it's this right leg of mine."

Me: "What's wrong with your leg?"

Her: "It's an artificial leg."

Me: "What happened?"

Her: "Oh, when I was three, I had cancer and they had to amputate my leg."

Great works are performed not by strength but by perseverance.

–Samuel Johnson

What were the chances? Of all the days, of all the planes, and of all the seats why was this young woman sitting next to me? For the second time that day I was stunned. The anger and frustration began to dissolve as I tried to understand what could be happening, what it meant.

She was a most willing listener as I shared the events of my day. Amazed, too, at the meaningful coincidence, she said all that I needed to hear. The possibilities for her own life were without question expanded significantly by the example of someone such as Terry Fox. "Please don't give up" were her parting words.

The next day, in a calmer, more positive frame of mind, I reviewed the Cancer Society's requests and realized that they were of a reasonable, legal nature, and with patience and flexibility I could satisfy them. Even so, after yesterday's experience, I knew the thought of giving up would never more be entertained.

Six months later the project was complete, and now *The Power of Purpose* is used by schools, colleges, nonprofits, and businesses throughout the world. A teacher showed the film to a group of sixth graders. She then asked them to write down an answer to the question, What did you learn from this film? Here is the reply of one child: "What I learned was when your leg is amputated, your spirit isn't."

The purpose for which the film was made is being fulfilled: The true legacy of Terry Fox lives on.

Concerning all acts of initiative (and creation), there is one elementary truth, the ignorance of which kills countless ideas and splendid plans; that the moment one definitely commits oneself, then Providence moves too. All sorts of things occur to help one that would never otherwise have occurred. A whole stream of events issues from the decisions, raising in one's favor all manner of unforeseen incidents and meetings and material assistance, which no man could have dreamt would have come his way. I have learned a deep respect for one of Goethe's couplets: Whatever you can do, or dream you can, begin it. Boldness has genius, power and magic in it.

–W. H. Murray

Commitment has been defined as a serious promise, but that definition begs clarification. Serious is certainly sincere but not necessarily solemn. A serious commitment should not take the joy and fun out of life, leaving no room for spontaneity and laughter. This advice has helped me enormously: Take your dreams seriously but not yourself. My mother sowed that seed early on in my life, for she felt that one of the most important of life's survival skills was the ability to laugh at ourselves. Be aware, therefore, of the humor in your own idiosyncrasies, and let laughter be an integral part of your daily existence.

Understand also the important distinction between giving up and giving in. You have been exhorted to never give up on what you want for your life, but there could be many times on your journey when it is wise to give in. Terry Fox gave in to the forces of nature at the beginning of his run, but he never gave up on his dream because he knew the bad weather could not last forever. I learned to give in when my family returned to Australia, but I never gave up on getting them back.

Finally, remember that life presents itself just one day at time. Make your commitments in daily bite-sized chunks that can be assimilated without risk of mental indigestion. One brick at a time a house is built, one stone at a time a cathedral. One stroke at a time the artist paints, one day at a time the alcoholic recovers his life. Learn from yesterday, do well the tasks of today, and tomorrow will look after itself.

May you live all the days of your life.

–Jonathan Swift

You Must Be What You Can Be

Leaving a Legacy

Chapter 9

O n his seventy-fifth birthday, Jacques Cousteau was congratulated by people from all over the world. The famous and not so famous turned out in the thousands to celebrate his work. Characteristically he focused on the future: "To yakety-yak about the past is for me time lost." With the enthusiasm of a young man, he went on to say, "I do not feel age; I see something I want to do and I have to do it."

Cousteau's popularity is no accident. The accolades have been well earned. He has expanded significantly the knowledge we have of our planet and, in doing so, has made a major contribution to its well being. For his commitment and vision Cousteau deserves to be admired. Beyond admiration, however, I believe he has earned our respect for what he represents. He is a model for what we all seek: to create something of value, to accomplish something worthwhile.

There exists within each of us a longing to leave a legacy, some proof that we were here. We need to know that our lives were important, that somehow our being here mattered. We can attempt to stifle or ignore this desire, but we cannot escape it. As humans we are distinguished and defined by it.

Ernest Becker stated, "What we fear is not so much extinction, but extinction with insignificance." This is an unwarranted fear. For as nature creates nothing superfluous, so it equips us with what we

Every morning I wake up saying, "I'm still alive—a miracle." And so I keep pushing.

–Jacques Cousteau

need to leave our legacy: the creative power of human intelligence. The primary purpose of this intelligence is to create something of value, to accomplish something worthwhlle. The evidence of this is in the evolution of our species. Where civilization stands today is the culmination of numerous creative acts by those who used their intelligence to improve the quality of human existence.

Marva Collins has spent her entire career as an educator. Her dissatisfaction with the "system" led her to start her own school on the West Side of Chicago in the fall of 1975. The outstanding results of her work have gained Marva international recognition Including a movie about her life. Marva Collins sums up her legacy this way: "I've desperately tried to make a difference in the world. I tell the kids in my school, 'I know I'm going to live forever through you.'"

We cannot live by the past; the present is so transient that it almost does not exist. As a matter of fact, we live by the future; or more accurately, we are unceasingly preparing ourselves toward it, trying to anticipate it, and from this process flow all new ideas. It is impossible to be alive without the effort to create and bring something new into concrete manifestation.

–Nicolai Fechin

What do you want to create?

Warren Buffet is recognized as a person of high integrity and principles. He has also created one of the most successful businesses in the world. Over a twenty-five year period, he took the per-share book value of his company, Berkshire Hathaway, from $19.46 to $4,296.01. Buffet gave an insight into his methods and philosophy in a Berkshire Hathaway annual report. Commenting on leveraged buy-outs, he said, "Leverage just moves things along faster. . . . I have never been in a big hurry. We enjoy the process far more than the proceeds, though we have learned to live with those also."

Gary Player described his reaction as Jack Nicklaus, having just turned fifty, played in his first PGA Seniors tournament: "I was in awe. You had to see it to believe it. He was fantastic." Nicklaus said, "Maybe I'll play well [today]. Maybe I'll win. Maybe I won't play well and won't win. But whatever happens, I'll learn something from it."

In a *Newsday* article, Irene Sax writes about Jean Nidetch, the founder of Weight Watchers, which has over one million members in twenty-four countries. In answer to Sax's question of why she has been able to help so many people, Nidetch tells of how she regularly crossed a park when she was a teenager and watched mothers chatting while their toddlers sat on swings with no one to push them. "I'd give them a push," she said. "And you know what happens when you push a kid on a swing? Pretty soon he's pumping, doing it himself. That's what my role in life is—I'm there to give others a push."

George Burns, on his 94th birthday, was asked if he felt he would live to be 100. He answered, "I have to, I'm booked."

Perhaps your ambitions are more modest than people such as these. But from their often humble beginnings, from their beliefs and values, and from what they have been able to create, there is much to learn. It is not only to the famous, however, that I owe my conviction about our creative ability. It is rooted more in the lives of the "ordinary" people I have been privileged to know but who are outstanding models of the creative process. With imagination, courage, and commitment, they have transcended doubt, fear, and insecurity to achieve extraordinary levels of personal fulfillment and prosperity.

This book has been an attempt to document what they have taught me. The timeless principles we have discussed are the tools with which they have created their lives. Although the trends and eccentricities of this changing world pass, these principles remain forever true. They are always reliable, always dependable, always functional. With them you can create a masterpiece.

Let us endeavor so to live that when we come to die even the undertaker will be sorry.

–Mark Twain